Garden
Wildlife

Garden Wildlife

The living world of your garden

Introduction by Derek Jones
Illustrated by Phil Weare

EBURY PRESS
London

For Holly Rose

Published by Ebury Press Limited
National Magazine House
72 Broadwick Street
LONDON W1V 2BP

First impression 1981
© Marshall Cavendish Limited 1981

ISBN 0 85223 213 6

Produced by
Marshall Cavendish Books Limited
58 Old Compton Street
LONDON W1V 5PA

Designed by Elizabeth Rose and Brenda Morrison

Printed in Italy

The publishers are grateful to Eyre Methuen Ltd. for
permission to quote from *King Solomon's Ring* by
Konrad Lorenz.

Introduction

A COUPLE OF YEARS ago there was a bit of a mystery when the milk man was leaving either too much milk or none at all. There was no explanation—the indicator was left outside the back door every night, either inside an empty bottle or leaning against the doorstep. Then I discovered that it was only on the nights when the indicator wasn't in the empty bottle that the order went wrong—something was moving it. Was there a secret agent of the Milk Marketing Board on the prowl, anxious to increase sales? As it happened, sales did increase, because when I had tracked down the culprit, my milk bill doubled during the summer months! The phantom mover was a hedgehog taking his nightly stroll and, ever nosey, turning over anything which might hide a meal.

So, having made the discovery that hedgehogs used the garden, I set about encouraging them by putting out a couple of dishes of milk every night, and I have never for one moment regretted that decision. Now I only have to go out just about the time when dusk is deepening, rattle the dishes, fill them with milk—and within five minutes there is a hedgehog lapping away with tiny darting tongue, and not satisfied until it has turned the dish on end by putting its front paws into it to get the last drop of milk. Of course, there was soon more than one hedgehog. Last summer a complete family turned up, and once the three youngsters had been introduced to the 'dining out' procedure, they would come along independently—and usually earlier than the sow or boar. Oddly, garden slugs like milk too, and it is quite usual to see a brave slug daringly draped over one side of the dish and a hedgehog slurping away at the other. The snag is that when I am feeding the hedgehogs they lose their appetite for slugs and my garden does not get cleared of them! But the pleasure they have given me has been beyond measure.

One day I rescued a tiny buddleia from the base of a wall in the BBC car park. It was all of two inches high at the time, but in the nourishing surroundings of the garden it flourished and I look out on it today and wonder if it will grow any taller than the present 15 feet. What a splendid plant to have in a corner of the garden. In that hot summer of 1976, seventeen different species of butterfly came to that buddleia, as well as a humming bird hawk-moth. Not a bad return for rescuing a tiny tree. Then, in the winter, birds find the buddleia seed-heads a good source of food and for the past four years those charming migrant warblers, blackcaps, have been regular visitors in the months of the year when we might have expected them to be in warmer climes. But yes, there are over-wintering blackcaps, and I am glad to have them in my garden. It is not only on the buddleia that they find their food: another favourite is honeysuckle with its shiny black berries. But top of the blackcap menu is the ornamental crab-apple which has its roots next door and hangs over my wall; the fruit are hard as bullets until the first frosts and then the blackcaps excavate them for the seeds, although last year they had to share with fieldfares. I have to warn any visitors during the summer not to worry about the sawing noise outside the bathroom window.

Up there, under the gable-end, are two house martins' nests and the young keep up constant contact calls all through the night. It is a sound very much like that made by a grasshopper warbler, a sound of summer—and I always calculate that summer has arrived every year when I hear the first excited twitterings of a pair of martins investigating the old nests under the roof; to me, it's as evocative as the first cry of a new-born baby—a proclamation of the continuity of life.

My garden, then, although small and village bound, is not just for me: it is for any wildlife that cares to share it with me. To help, I always leave a corner of nettles for the butterflies that need them; the compost heap is not disturbed in the spring until any hedgehogs that might have holed up there for the winter have emerged; pruning is left until any useful seeds have ended up as food for the birds; and who cares if the shape of leaves on the rose bushes has been re-fashioned by leaf-cutting bees? Every day my garden gives me a new surprise, new pleasure. It is not just a garden really—it is a tiny nature reserve.

This book, written by a group of highly qualified naturalists, some of whom I know as personal friends, underlines what efforts we can all make to attract birds, butterflies, bees, mammals, reptiles and other creatures into our gardens. Anything we can do to provide even the tiniest haven is important when so many species are under pressure—under pressure from *us* because of *our* needs. When we take we must also give, otherwise our world will be a sadder, emptier place.

Contents

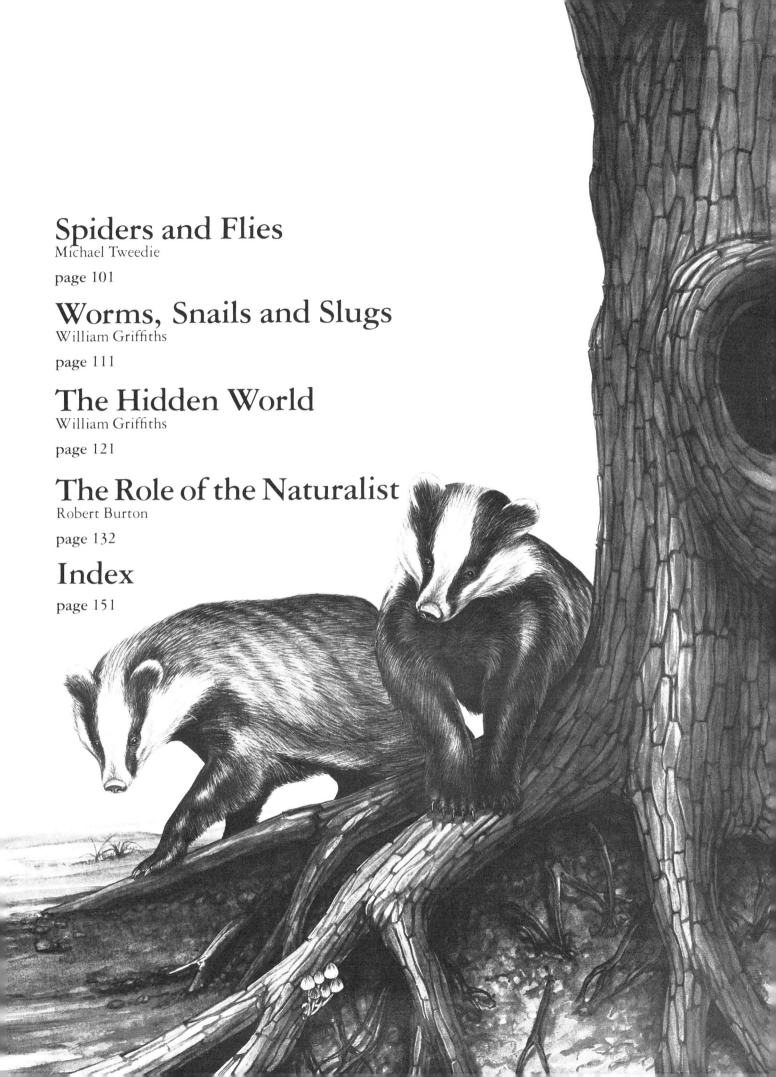

The Garden Environment

The most important factors in determining the character of a garden environment are the attitudes and objectives of the gardener. Historically, man's first efforts at plant cultivation were for the production either of food or medicines (one of the oldest garden sites in London is that of the Chelsea Physic Garden which dates back to 1673). Even so, gardens purely for pleasure are known to have been maintained around the Tigris and Euphrates rivers in Mesopotamia 7000 years ago. What has always been evident is that, while in an agricultural situation man must restrict himself to growing food plants, as soon as he has had the opportunity of plant husbandry for pleasure, he has experimented gladly with different species and methods of cultivation.

In the seventeenth century, it became fashionable to introduce exotic species from overseas, and gardeners strove to improve nature by breeding larger and more colourful flowers; such exercises were to shape much of the character of the larger, more formal English gardens and were also to influence the smaller urban plots. The first recorded plant collection trip from Britain was made by John Tradescant who was the Earl of Salisbury's head gardener. In 1609 he left Hatfield, the Salisbury estate in Hertfordshire, and visited much of Europe in search of new species. Later, when he worked for the Duke of Buckingham, his influence was so great that he was able to arrange for the Royal Navy to bring back plants from overseas.

The mid eighteenth century saw a boom in landscape gardening, pioneered by 'Capability' Brown who, in 1751, was able to set up in London as a sort of freelance consultant garden architect to the aristocracy. There was a tremendous increase, too, in the number of species being introduced into the country as a result of work by both the Royal Botanic Gardens at Kew and the Royal Horticultural Society. The trend continued into the early part of the next century with the introduction, by David Douglas, of many conifers from North America to supplement our three national species, the Scots pine, the yew and the juniper. If you visit your nearest park you will probably see examples of some of the conifers first brought into Britain by Douglas. During the latter part of the nineteenth century another pioneer, Joseph Hooker, sent home thirty species of rhododendron from India—until that time the plant was almost unknown in this country; now most parks contain at least one species in their shrub borders. In all, it has been estimated that at least 850 new plant species were introduced into Britain between 1850 and 1950, so the chances of your own garden environment being influenced by non-indigenous plants is very high; even if you were to plant only native species, windblown or bird-spread seeds of one or two introductions would almost certainly appear.

The spread of the railway system towards the end of the nineteenth century made it possible to get out of towns into the countryside. At the same time, there was growing interest in natural history and it became fashionable for the urban gardener to dig up native wild plants and take them back home to the garden: the rarer the plant the more desirable it was. Some species have become so threatened by collection that legislation has been passed to protect all wild plants, including 'weeds'. It is an offence, under the Conservation of Wild Creatures and Wild Plants Act 1975, for anyone, other than an authorized person, to uproot any plant. 'Authorized person' means the landowner, the occupier or someone authorized by them. The same Act also protects twenty-one named rare species from picking or destruction except when this is done in accordance with 'good agricultural practice'.

In recent times, the success of natural history programmes on television, pioneered by the BBC *Look* series, introduced by Peter Scott in the 1950s, has done much to foster a general appreciation of, and interest in, British wildlife. Obviously, some groups of animals gain more public sympathy than others: a prime example is the phenomenal success and influence of the Royal Society for the Protection of Birds (RSPB). Thanks largely to the work of this Society, many people encourage birds to come into their gardens by the use of nest boxes and feeding tables, and legislation protecting wild birds is far more comprehensive than that covering any other animal group. Over the years, the attitudes of many gardeners have changed from

Rhododendrons are one of the many kinds of plants brought from foreign places to enhance British parks and gardens. They are related to the heathers, and most of the 600 species come from the mountainous regions of Asia, although some originate from North America. Like many introduced plants, they harbour few insects in their new home, but clumps of rhododendrons provide nesting places for birds in summer. They are used as roosts by redwings and greenfinches in winter.

what might be described as the Man versus Nature approach, through Man with Nature, to a view of Man as a part of Nature—a view expressed for many in the successful television series, *The Good Life*.

All forms of gardening are, to a certain extent, a fight against nature since, if she had her way, she would, by a process known as succession, turn most of Britain into mixed deciduous woodland dominated by oak trees. A knowledge of the basic working of this process, whereby even a bare rock surface can eventually support trees, is valuable for anybody concerned with any form of land management. The process can be broken down into several distinct stages, and an examination of any garden will normally show signs of it in action.

THE ONLY PLANTS able to grow on bare rocks are very simple ones, such as lichens and mosses. A lichen is, in fact, a dual plant which is composed of a fungus living with an alga. Neither could live on their own on a rock surface but, by working in cooperation, they are able to survive as if they were a single plant. Although it is a little-known group, lichen species outnumber flowering plant species in the British flora and they are of great value as biological indicators of air pollution.

When these initial pioneer plants die, their own decomposed organic remains, together with trapped windblown particles of soil, eventually form a substrate in which broad-leaved weeds, such as dandelions and plantains, can gain a hold. Once the broad-leaved weeds start to spread, the remaining pioneer species are practically obscured. Any keen gardener will confirm that weeds are able to colonize any bare scrap of soil: in the natural process of succession, they play a valuable role in building up soil structure and, in particular, humus content, thereby creating the conditions required by plants which the gardener may well regard with a little more affection.

The broad-leaved weeds are eventually shaded out by invading grasses, which will, in turn, eventually be replaced by scrub species such as bramble, hawthorn and elder. Anybody who doubts this should try not mowing the lawn for a year! The climax of the successional process is when the tallest of plants—that is, trees— become dominant and a woodland habitat results.

In Britain the dominant tree would eventually be the oak since at the present time the climate and soil conditions over most of the country favour it above all other native trees. Exceptions to this rule are in the far north and at high altitudes, where Scots pine or birch would be better able to survive, on steep chalk slopes where beech would be more successful, and in marshy areas where alders and willows would be the dominant tree species. In the latter case, however, the alders and willows would eventually be replaced by oak as the ground dried out. During the last Ice Age, pine was probably dominant but by about 8000 BC the ice was retreating and by 5000 BC the climate was suitable for a takeover by the oaks. In the year 1 AD, Britain must have been largely covered by oak forests and, but for man's need for fuel, timber, grazing and arable farm lands, that might well still have been the situation today. Since oaks have been growing in Britain for thousands of years, it is not surprising that more than 280 species of insects have learnt to live on them. As a general rule, introduced plants do not support nearly as many animal species as do native ones, a point that can be readily appreciated by examining the foliage of a sycamore tree in the summer. The sycamore was introduced into Britain about 500 years ago and only a few insects have adapted to using it as a food plant. During the summer months sycamores will carry many thousands of greenfly but little else; you would be hard pressed to find more than ten species living on one tree. Since it does not carry the range of predators that the oak does, the number of sap-sucking aphids on a single tree can build up to plague proportions. Unfortunately, the winged 'helicopter' seeds of the sycamore are spread over a wide area by the wind and, since the trees cast a deep shade, very little can be grown beneath them. So you can see that sycamores will suppress not only fauna but flora as well, and many conservationists regard them as weeds. If you want to attract a wide range of animals into your garden you would certainly be well advised to think about removing any seedling sycamores and replacing them with one or two oaks.

LTHOUGH EACH OF the five successional stages—that is, pioneers, broad-leaved weeds, grasses, scrub and woodland— supports its own characteristic fauna and flora, each works to the same basic ecological blueprint. All living organisms require energy, and they can be broadly classified into groups according to where and how they obtain it.

Green plants obtain their energy by photosynthesis, the process whereby radiant energy from the Sun is converted into a form of chemical energy which can be used by the plant. In effect, every green leaf can be regarded as a factory which produces sugars whenever sunlight falls on it. The first link in any food chain is the Sun. The second is a green plant which converts the Sun's energy into a chemical form which is usable, not only by the plant itself, but also by plant-eating animals and saprophytic plants, such as fungi, which cannot produce their own food by photosynthesis. Because of their primary role in food chains, green plants are collectively known as producers while plant-eating animals are known as herbivores. The third link in a food chain is some form of herbivore which may range in size from a sap-sucking aphid, or even smaller, up to an elephant. The final links are composed of one or more carnivorous or meat-eating animals.

Wherever there is life on earth, a system based on simple food chains can be seen in operation: a food chain in your garden, for example, might be as follows:

SUN........CABBAGE...............SLUG...............SLOW-WORM
 (Producer)   (Herbivore)   (Carnivore)

Over a period of many years, bare rock is transformed into forests of tall trees. When the country emerged from the ice ages, the ground had been scraped bare by the glaciers. The first plants to arrive were lichens which clung tenaciously to bare rock. They were followed by such simple plants as mosses, liverworts and ferns which grew in crevices where dirt and debris from weathered rock had gathered.

Over the centuries, the decomposed remains of the plants gathered until there was sufficient soil for the seeds of flowering plants to germinate and grow. At first they would have been low herbs of the kind which become weeds in gardens, they are called colonisers because of their ability to appear and grow on bare soil. Eventually taller herbs, shrubs and, finally, trees take over. The series of plants is called succession. Early stages can be seen on old buildings, where lichens, mosses and weeds take root or on waste ground where scrub is encroaching.

It is interesting to work out what would happen to any link in the above food chain if the population of any of the other links were either to increase or decrease to any extent. Making such calculations is a help in understanding the concept of a natural balance in nature. The exercise can be extended if one lists all the other things in the garden that eat cabbage, are eaten by slugs, eat slugs, are eaten by slow-worms, or even eat slow-worms. The results should give some idea as to how simple food chains do not, in reality, exist in isolation but rather criss-cross to form complex webs. Since your own garden will contain many more green plants than just cabbages, you can see how complicated a food web picture even the smallest garden can be.

A common feature of all the living links in any food web is that they eventually die, and it is an interesting thought that without death there could be no life. In order to survive, green plants require not only an energy input from the Sun but also a supply of chemical nutrients from the soil. These nutrients are supplied largely by the actions of organisms of decay, such as fungi and bacteria, which obtain their energy by breaking down organic material. To a certain extent, a deciduous tree can be said to be cannibalistic, since its roots obtain vital nutrients from its own rotting leaves.

You and your garden are a small part of an extremely complex biological system through which energy flows, and around which nutrients are continually cycling; provided that the living organisms that go to make up this system are in balance, it could go on operating

successfully for millions of years to come, until the day that the Sun eventually dies.

A small example of how an imbalance can occur can be seen if we consider the story of two rival rose growers who both had a blackfly problem. The first grower sprayed his garden with an insecticide and the second did nothing. After two weeks, the first grower had a far worse problem on his hands while the second seemed to have the problem under control. How can one explain this when it was the first grower who had taken steps to combat the blackfly? The answer lies in the amazing life cycle of the blackfly which over-winters as an egg from which a female hatches in the spring. When a few days old, the first female gives birth to a daughter and continues to do so every few days throughout her life. The daughters likewise give birth every few days, so you can see why the potential annual offspring from a single egg is well over five and a half million; if you examine a cluster of blackfly with a magnifying glass you will quite likely see at least one offspring being born. As autumn approaches, the females start to give birth to males as well as females so that mating can take place in order for fertile eggs to be produced to over-winter ready for the next spring hatching. It has been calculated that in the space of two years, the potential offspring from a single egg could devour all of the terrestrial green plants on this planet and so bring life on land to a halt. The reason why this destructive potential is never fully realized is, of course, that there are many animals that eat blackfly and so keep the population in check. Can you work out why rose grower number one came off worse? The answer is that blackfly breeds at a much faster rate than its predators which were also killed off by the insecticide.

The incident involving the two rose growers happened a few years ago and there are now selective insecticides available that kill only pest species and do not affect beneficial insects, other than by removing a large part of their food supply. What happens if the beneficial insect populations drop through lack of food and the pest species develop an immunity to selective insecticides is a matter for speculation. It is as if those animals which produce large numbers of offspring do so because they know that most of their young will never live to maturity.

The chain of life, or the hunters and the hunted. Plants get their energy from the sun by the process of photosynthesis and all animals eventually depend on plants for food. Plant-eating animals form the food of carnivorous animals and this picture shows the links in a food-chain which may be seen in the garden. The slugs are feeding on grass. They provide food for the shrew which will, itself, sustain the waiting weasel.

15

Despite the large number of eggs in a clump of frog spawn, for example, we are never overrun with adult frogs. Most birds manage to produce more than two fledglings per pair but, despite this, bird populations remain fairly constant in a balanced system.

A key to maintaining biological stability is to ensure that there is a large diversity of species on earth; if any species becomes extinct, without being naturally replaced by the process of evolution, the chances of a biological breakdown are increased. How can you use your garden to help maintain a large diversity of animal and plant species?

There is a lot of truth in the conservationist saying, 'Look after the habitat and the animals will look after themselves'. In order to enrich your garden environment with a wide diversity of fauna and flora, it is useful to regard it as a mosaic of habitats, each supporting a variety of plant and animal species. If there is enough space, long and short grass areas of lawn will support a wider variety of species than either long or short grass on its own. If left unattended, any lawn will eventually be invaded and then dominated by scrub and so some form of lawn management is obviously essential. Three basic methods are possible: grazing, burning or mowing. Grazing by sheep or controlled burning may be possible on large national nature reserves but for normal garden purposes, mowing is obviously the only practical answer. Before you decide on your mowing régime, however, it is essential to ask yourself what you require as an end-product of your labours. If you decide that you want a short lawn with one variety of grass, there are many books on lawn management to advise you, but if you decide that you want a wild flower lawn, advice is not so easily obtainable. Possibly the most important thing to aim for is a lowering of the nutrient status of the soil under the lawn, so do not add fertilizers and *do* remove all cuttings. If you leave grass cuttings to rot down, the effect will be the same as if you had added fertilizers—one or two dominant species will shoot up and shade out everything else.

I T IS QUITE definitely the attitude and objectives of the gardener which determine the character of the garden environment. I worked for several years for a Royal Society for the Prevention of Cruelty to Animals (RSPCA) Emergency Service Team in the London area, and saw much that illustrated attitudes towards gardens and wildlife in general.

I am pleased that my own garden is visited by hedgehogs: they are not only interesting and attractive animals in their own right but they keep down garden pests. This 'live and let live' philosophy is totally different from that of the lady who made an emergency call to the RSPCA to report that she had a hedgehog on her lawn. She demanded that the RSPCA 'do something': come and remove or destroy this invader of her territory so that she could let her children out to play again. She was most upset that the animal had ventured into her garden; nobody could convince her that garden boundaries only have significance for humans, and that wild fauna and flora would not be at

The natterjack toad is protected by law but the sandy places where it lives are disappearing. It may come into gardens surrounding its few remaining refuges, but elsewhere gardens are becoming important sanctuaries where other amphibians can safely spawn in ponds.

all deterred by a line marked on the deeds of her property.

Are you willing to share your garden with the local wildlife or would you—say—complain about the dawn chorus and demand that someone comes and lays poisons to kill the birds?

If you do want to share your garden, it is important that you do not become too tidy-minded. A man once complained bitterly that his favourite wild robin had suddenly stopped visiting him. It transpired that he had recently had a grand tidy-up session and when he was told that his robin had not been calling to see him personally, but rather to feed on the host of mini-beasts which had lived in the wilder parts of his garden, he was most upset.

A garden habitat designed to encourage wildlife might include areas of long and short grass, a bramble or nettle patch, a weed bed, a few old logs left to rot down and—possibly most productive of all—a pond. The installation of a pond, be it a large expensive butyl rubber mini-lake or a washing-up bowl sunk into the lawn, will do more to encourage wildlife than almost anything else. A pond not only encourages birds and other land animals to visit your garden, but also opens the door to a wide range of aquatic insects, molluscs, crustacea, amphibia and so on.

It would be surprising if many gardens provided a refuge for rare species, but if the common species are not to become rare, it is essential for suitable habitats to be available to them and here gardens can play an important role. Only one British amphibian, the natterjack toad, is at present protected by law, but there is growing concern about the status of the crested newt and the common frog, both facing increasing problems when it comes to finding suitable

spawning sites. The urban garden pond is less likely to be polluted, collected from, or filled in than is the average rural one, and so it is not surprising that surveys of urban populations of ponds are often more encouraging than those carried out in the countryside.

In days gone by, if one wanted to study natural history, one visited the countryside, explored the hedgerows that made up the traditional patchwork quilt of the English countryside, and searched in pond and brook for interesting specimens. A by-product of traditional methods of agricultural plant and animal husbandry was a mosaic of habitats which supported a wide diversity of life. Modern, more productive agricultural practices have, in many cases, destroyed essential habitat types, and the time may not be too far off when naturalists turn to towns and town parks, and gardens as study areas. National and country parks do exist in the countryside but the pressures on them as amenity and recreational areas are tremendous. National nature reserves are, to a certain extent, protected but could become living museums of specimen habitat types where, for practical conservation purposes, access would need to be restricted. In order to be a viable proposition, a nature reserve needs to be reasonably large, and large tracts of the British countryside are in danger of being turned into a homogeneous mono-culture of the local crop. In contrast, an aerial photograph of a large area of urban gardens would show many individual plots each being managed according to the particular aims of the gardener concerned, but together adding up to an urban patchwork quilt: a mosaic of habitat types. The fact that the mosaic is composed of small units is a protection against the type of large-scale development that can be seen in the countryside. It could even be argued that, collectively, urban gardens have a greater potential in wildlife conservation than the largest of the national nature reserves.

TOWNS SUPPORT A surprisingly large range of wildlife and the study of how animals have adapted to an urban environment makes a very interesting topic. When and where did the first blue tit steal the top of the milk from a sealed bottle? The scavenging habits of the highly omnivorous town fox differ greatly from those of his more carnivorous country cousin. Given no more natural nesting site, a robin will successfully rear a family on the top of a lamp post or a bus stop, if it has an adequate supply of food. These and many more animals could easily appear in your garden. Information on the flora and fauna of your own area is normally freely available from local museums, natural history societies, county trusts for nature conservation, field clubs and other natural history or conservation organizations. Please remember to send a stamped addressed envelope with a query to any of these bodies. The RSPB or their Young Ornithologists Club, both based at The Lodge, Sandy, Bedfordshire would certainly be very pleased to supply details of different types of nest boxes or bird tables and other bird 'furniture' which you can obtain to attract wild birds to your garden reserve.

Birds

A garden with well-kept borders, neatly cut lawn, immaculate flower beds and a tidy appearance can look very attractive. To many human eyes, the whole effect is pleasing; to the eyes of most birds, however, such a garden may offer few opportunities for exploitation.

The main method of tempting wildlife into a garden is to increase the diversity of habitats the garden contains. This can be done by encouraging a wide variety of plants to grow which, in turn, will attract animal life, from birds to 'creepy crawlies'. There are, of course, limits to the range of different species you can expect to attract—for instance, the types of birds which can live in your garden will be determined mainly by the fact that it is essentially a woodland edge habitat, so only birds suited to this, or those that enjoy a close association with man, will live there. However, in many gardens there may be features uncharacteristic of woodlands which could attract non-woodland species: for example, the eaves of a house may provide the ideal nest site for house martins or swallows.

Generally speaking, gardens have their own list of bird species but as the garden grows and matures the list may increase as new resources become available for other species. I once lived in a house that had a very mature garden with tall trees and a thick growth of bushes and shrubs. Within this bird haven lived nuthatches and tawny owls and, during the summer, spotted flycatchers successfully reared their young.

By planting trees which grow to different heights, you may attract more species than if you leave the edges of the garden very low. Similarly, artificial structures will often satisfy the needs of visiting birds. For example, a bird table in the middle of the lawn can be like an oasis in the desert for members of the tit family. Being reluctant to alight on the grass, they prefer perches off the ground, and feel at home on the man-made table.

Only when a garden suits the needs of the bird will it choose to live there. A spotted flycatcher, for example, looking for its summer residence, evaluates a

Unlike the swift, swallow and martin which hawk through the air in search of flying insects, the flycatcher waits on a perch for an insect to approach. Then it flies out, seizes the insect and returns to the perch. If it nests, it can be watched as it takes its prey to the growing chicks.

habitat on the basis of several important features. Firstly, there has to be a hawking post—a tree branch, post or wall from which it can make fluttering attacks on unsuspecting passing insects. Secondly, there must be a secure nesting site, well protected, preferably in ivy climbing up the side of a house. Every species has its own requirements and no one garden can possibly fulfil the needs of every bird. But the more you can provide in terms of functional artificial and natural features, the greater the variety of birds that you will be privileged to watch visiting and staying in your garden.

Over a period of a full year in an average suburban garden, an observer may see something, in the region of twenty-five to thirty different types of birds. When conditions are particularly good, or when migrants pass through the garden, up to fifty species may be counted. One particularly skilled bird ringer trapped fifty-five species in his nets from one garden. Only about half of this number would normally be visible, as many species are naturally reticent. The main problem in trying to spot birds in the garden is that many only reveal themselves very early in the morning or are so shy that they spend most of their time lurking unseen among hedges and shrubbery.

Most birds become active immediately the sun rises, so by the time you have staggered out of bed and into breakfast, the birds which need to sing have already sung their territorial morning chorus and have reached the third course of their breakfast. They are at their busiest early in the morning and this, consequently, is the best time to observe them.

One of the most outstanding members of the garden community is the blackbird. Whether a garden is neat and tidy, overgrown with weeds or hardly planted, there will nearly always be a blackbird nearby. On the lawn it is a conspicuous sight as it scuttles along, then stops, watching intently for any slight movement which may give away the presence of a worm or some other tasty morsel. A garden must be the blackbird's favourite residential area: there are three times as many of them living in gardens as there are in woods. Suburban blackbirds tend to have a higher productivity rate than blackbirds in rural areas.

The song thrush, not quite so common as the blackbird, but very similar in habits, has a particularly outstanding reputation as a tool user. A thrush will use a piece of hard rock or concrete against which it batters the shell of snails in order to reach the tasty soft parts. I have seen three thrush's 'anvils' but have not so far been able to watch a bird using this tool. The thrush is territorial and its song is characterized by the repetition of a number of basic elements.

Snails are a favourite food of the song thrush. It opens them by smashing the shell against a stone or a concrete path. Favourite 'anvils' become littered with fragments of shells and the thrush can be watched at work if you listen for the sharp knock as it smashes open another victim.

OTHER GROUND-FEEDING birds in the garden are the dunnock and the starling. The dunnock, or hedge sparrow as it is sometimes called, is a relatively inconspicuous little brown bird that spends much of its time near the ground. It may venture out on to the lawn from time to time but stays close to vegetation in its search for small seeds and insects. The starling, on the other hand, is a noisy, almost showy bird that always draws attention to itself when out on the open lawn. It is extremely sociable by nature and will gather with other starlings, forming small feeding groups. Starlings will also roost together with several thousand birds congregating at a favoured place. They seem to be attracted by the warmth and shelter of the urban environment, so they roost willingly in towns and cities, 'commuting' out to gardens and the countryside in search of food.

Like the starling, other birds will use the lawn as a feeding ground and are consequently fairly noticeable. Song thrushes, chaffinches, robins and, of course, sparrows are all common. Pied wagtails and gulls occasionally make an appearance, too. Wood pigeons and collared doves land on the lawn mostly when food to their liking is put out. Pigeons and doves have always struck me as rather gentle, attractive birds, but many people dislike them for the damage they do to plants and vegetable crops. They do, however, have a charm of their own and are worth encouraging into the garden.

For the past ten years the collared dove has rapidly established itself as a successful species in this country. There was a time when its hunting call was unusual enough to make the bird watcher turn and watch but now the sound is too familiar to warrant more than a glance. Its expansion into new areas is a total success story for a bird that was a rare sight thirty years ago. I encourage our local pair down on to the lawn by leaving out corn meal—a mixture of barley, wheat and maize.

21

A lawn has the great advantage of being a natural arena where birds display and behave in full view of even the most casual of bird watchers. However, although it is a marvellous place for some birds, for many others it is potentially hazardous, offering very little in the way of protection and therefore to be avoided. In fact, some birds are positively agoraphobic, preferring to remain in or under bushes. The wren is one of them. Normally, it is reluctant to show itself in the open but during severe weather conditions it will do so temporarily, out of desperation to find food. Throughout the worst of the 1978–9 winter, a wren living in my garden would come very close to my house, seeking the invertebrate life living in the moss growing on the vertical face of the patio, which was sheltered and free from snow. Very hard winters claim the lives of many wrens. Before the 1978–9 winter, it was among the four most common birds in Great Britain but now the numbers seem to have dropped drastically and it may well be some years before they return to anything like their previous level.

NOWHERE NEAR AS shy as the wren, the more common members of the tit family eagerly visit gardens but dislike being on the lawn or close to the ground. They live at a level several feet from the ground and prefer not to descend if they can avoid it. The most regular visitors are the blue and great tits but sometimes the coal tit also puts in an appearance, particularly when there is a convenient conifer tree in which to set up home. Although all tits move and feed above the ground, they are quite visible, and their colours and inquisitive behaviour make them attractive and entertaining to watch.

In fact, tits have really taken advantage of the facilities that man provides: those that have difficulty in obtaining a foothold in their natural woodland habitat can resort to artificial nest boxes and the sustaining fare of the bird table. But what appears to be an ideal way of life may have its drawbacks, for this species lays large numbers of eggs, averaging about thirteen per clutch. Parent blue tits living in woodland could expect to rear a reasonable number of youngsters, because the hatching of the eggs coincides with the greatest availability of their food source, a variety of caterpillar which feeds on oak leaves. The lack of an adequate supply of such caterpillars in the garden makes feeding the young an arduous task for the parents and many of the brood may die of starvation if food resources are low that year. Blue tit populations are apt to fluctuate, so it is probably worth encouraging them to nest in your garden to help to increase the population. Sometimes those that visit the garden may be part of a transient population, temporarily sampling the delights of the bird table, only to move off the next day to some other location.

THE ROBIN IS another popular garden bird. It is renowned for its ability to take advantage of invertebrate prey turned up when somebody is digging the soil, and the friendliness it shows towards humans makes it an endearing companion. It is, however, by no means as friendly to other robins and during the breeding season a male will staunchly defend his territory against other intruding males. Although frequently visible in the garden—except in July, the time of its feather moult—the robin tends not to venture too far out on to the lawn, making only short food-gathering sorties into the open.

A bird which comes low in the popularity stakes is the house sparrow. It is dull to look at, and can sometimes cause offence by driving away more desirable species from the garden—so it is no

Robins were voted the national bird of Britain because of their friendly habits. They readily follow on the heels of the gardener to feed on worms and insects turned up by the fork, and a few become bold enough to hop indoors through open windows and doors. The habit of visiting gardeners is a development of the robins' natural behaviour of following large forest animals to catch insects turned up by their hooves.

The song of the robin can be heard throughout the winter. The pairs split up and male and female defend their own territories. Even the female sings, an unusual accomplishment for her sex.

The chances of having birds nesting in the garden are improved if some attention is paid to the way that shrubs are pruned. This is best carried out when the shrubs are young and the leaves have fallen. The arrangement of branches needs to be carefully examined and the effect on the overall shape of the bush taken into account before work starts. The aim is to produce two or three limbs diverging from a central point so that a nest can be slung between them as safely as if held in a cupped hand. The nearer the centre of the shrub the better, because this will give the birds the best cover from the elements and predators.

wonder it has few supporters. And yet this bird has to be congratulated on its ability to turn up here, there and everywhere: wherever there is man and his food, in Great Britain anyway, there will almost certainly be a house sparrow nearby.

ANOTHER GROUP THAT frequents gardens is the finch family. All garden finches, the chaffinch, bullfinch, greenfinch and goldfinch, are very attractive to look at, and every effort should be made to attract them. The chaffinch is among the four most common birds in Great Britain and can be seen all year round in the garden but especially during the winter. It is a strongly territorial bird during the breeding season, which is connected to the fact that young chaffinches are fed exclusively on invertebrates. By covering a large territory the parent chaffinch can ensure an adequate supply of food for all the hungry youngsters.

Greenfinches are increasing in number thanks to their enthusiasm for eating the peanuts that are often left in the garden to attract birds. Although it is not as dexterous as a blue tit on a hanging bag of peanuts, the greenfinch is always an attractive bird to watch.

Bullfinches and goldfinches are less common than the other finches. For some people, this is no bad thing as the damage done by the bullfinch to the buds of fruit trees and other carefully nurtured plants can be devastating. More sympathetic gardeners should forget this destructive trait and think only of the striking pink, black and grey plumage of this bird, which makes it one of the most beautifully coloured species in the country. The goldfinch is altogether less destructive, since it takes seeds rather than buds, and mainly from plants that are generally regarded as weeds. It, too, is brightly coloured, and a large flock of goldfinches flitting and twittering along in search of food is a marvellous spectacle.

One of the most intelligent of birds to be found in gardens is the nuthatch. It is small and slatey grey with a prominent dark streak on its head. Being a woodland bird, it prefers a more mature garden and will take advantage of food put out on local bird tables. It may use nest boxes, but it is not a particularly common garden bird. If you are, in fact, fortunate enough to have a local nuthatch, its bright and perky behaviour makes it a particularly interesting bird for you to watch.

The number of individual birds and, for that matter, the number of species present in the garden, whether they are residential or visiting, will vary throughout the year. The factors which determine this variation are many and include weather conditions, seasonal changes, food availability, reproduction and behavioural mechanisms. Most of the time, these factors interact with each other, causing local fluctuations in numbers. Weather conditions may affect the actual number which you see in the garden at any one time. For example, during winter some birds from a wide catchment area tend to gather together around a feeding point and new or unusual species may join them. Under harsh conditions, birds such as the reed bunting have been known to come to gardens in search of food.

Seasonal changes will affect food availability for certain birds, and many will, of course, migrate to or from an area. Summer brings spotted flycatchers, house martins, swallows, swifts and several species of warblers. All these birds arrive in Britain to feed on the myriad insects and rear their youngsters on this rich food supply. Probably only the house martin will be common in gardens, nesting under the eaves of a house and feeding on the aerial prey floating a hundred feet above us. If you have nesting house martins this year, expect them next year too, as they are creatures of habit, returning to familiar haunts.

Autumn and winter bring their migrants too—the fieldfare and the redwing, thrushlike birds that prefer open areas such as parks and playing fields. The fieldfare may come into gardens in search of berries and insects, and greatly appreciates any spare, damaged or windfallen fruit. Only rarely will a redwing visit a garden.

THE BREEDING SEASON has a direct effect on the number of birds in the garden, both before the season begins, when they are pairing up, and at the end, when the young birds are recruited into the population. At this time behavioural mechanisms have a prominent influence. For example, normally social species, such as the starling, flock together, but during the breeding season they pair up and spread themselves out evenly, seeking nest sites.

Birds that are territorial become particularly aggressive during the breeding season, fighting off intruders. Robins, dunnocks, thrushes, blackbirds and chaffinches all jostle with others of their own species for their piece of territory. Once the perimeter of each territory is established, the birds busily set about the business of breeding and defending their own precious area. The bird song that you hear in the morning and evening is a daily declaration of such ownership and if this long-distance signalling is insufficient to prevent intrusion by other individuals of the same species, the owner of the territory may have to resort to body signalling or even do battle with the intruder. The owner will normally win such a battle. This type of behaviour can often be seen, particularly among blackbirds. During the winter, such aggressive attitudes almost disappear and erstwhile enemies gather together over any food supply that can be found.

When the birds have finally bred and reared their youngsters, the offspring may be driven from the territory by their parents or they may take the place of adult birds when they die, and continue to use the garden habitat.

If you wish to attract particular species of birds, it is worth considering the types of food which each one enjoys. In general, birds, like other animals, fall into three main categories in their feeding habits: herbivores, carnivores and omnivores. Each bird species, however, can have a far wider choice of food than do other animals, so

By looking at the beak, it is possible to get a good idea of what a bird eats. The two main types of beaks among garden birds are the stout triangular beaks of seed-eaters and the slender beaks of insect-eaters.

Finches and sparrows are seed-eaters and they use their strong beaks for cracking the shell of seeds, but they do not feed wholly on seeds. Most feed their growing young on protein-rich insects and the bullfinch, shown here, eats buds in spring when there is a shortage of seeds. The tits, robin and wren are the most common insect-eaters. They use their tweezer-like beaks for plucking insects off plants or the ground. The tree creeper has a long bill for probing down crevices in bark. The swallows, swifts and martins catch flying insects in a wide mouth. Crows, jays, magpies, blackbirds and thrushes have general purpose beaks which are used for plucking fruit, probing the soil for invertebrates, pecking small insects, pulling at carrion and so on.

these categories tend to overlap and blur. In fact, many zoologists prefer to divide most birds into two separate groups: the hardbills, which are essentially seed-eaters, and the softbills which include both fruit-eaters and insect-eaters. It is best for our purposes to use these divisions, adding to them birds of prey and the carrion feeders of the crow family.

The shape of the beak reflects the diet of the bird. Those that have short, stout beaks are the hardbilled seed-eaters. The obvious seed-eaters which visit the garden include the bullfinch (which also eats flower buds, often causing great damage to fruit trees), the greenfinch, goldfinch and chaffinch. The beak of the goldfinch is more pointed than that of the bullfinch or greenfinch and is used for plucking out the seeds which lie deep in the heads of thistles, dandelions and groundsel. Because the cock goldfinch has a larger beak than the hen, he is more adept at extracting food from plants such as teasels, which have seeds set far down in the seed-head. Most of the finch family are particularly well adapted for seed eating, especially the crossbill, whose upper and lower mandibles are crossed at the ends to make it easier to extract seeds from pine cones. Because the crossbill feeds on pine seeds, it is restricted to living in pine forests and and has a limited distribution in Britain. At the other extreme from the crossbill is the chaffinch, which is nowhere near as specialized in its choice of food. It has a narrow beak and eats seeds of many sizes and also insects. Because of this varied diet it is widely distributed throughout the country. To the softbill category of birds belong those species which feed on everything from fruit to invertebrates, including worms, spiders, caterpillars, slugs, butterflies, moths, wood-lice and ants (particularly relished by the green woodpecker). They are specifically adapted for feeding upon invertebrates: as a group, the insectivorous birds have beaks which tend to be long and thin, and designed like a pair of tweezers so that the bird can probe and poke out insects from a hiding place and grip them tightly. Smaller birds, such as wrens, may have such tiny beaks that they can only pick up the minutest invertebrate life, most of which seems almost invisible to the naked human eye. Bigger insect-eaters tend to eat larger insects but, surprisingly, the song thrush enjoys feeding on greenfly, which must rate as a delicacy for such a comparatively large bird. The range in beak size allows different species to exploit different sizes of prey within the same area and therefore to avoid direct competition for food.

The tree creeper is an example of probably the most extreme beak development in an insect-eating British bird. This small, brown species is seen in mature gardens, scuttling up trees from the base, working its way round and probing with its long, curved beak into any rocks and crannies in the bark to extract insects and their larvae.

Martins, swallows and swifts are also insectivorous, but they have wide beaks rather than long, thin narrow ones. The advantage of this type of structure is that the bird can fly swiftly and easily through the mass of aerial plankton, composed of millions of insects living high in the air, gathering beakfuls of food.

Many softbills are omnivorous, feeding on both plant and animal material. Small invertebrates, seeds and many fruits are extremely nutritious, and because birds cannot fly well if they are laden with a gut full of bulky food, they opt in the main for a diet of either seeds or insects or the two mixed with fruits. They could not survive in Britain if they were exclusively fruit-eaters, mainly because fruit is available only in certain seasons. For the same reason, some insectivorous birds, such as swallows, martins, swifts and some warblers, have to migrate to find a continual supply of insects.

Members of the crow family are omnivores, feeding on just about anything from fruit to carrion. The jay and magpie are the most common garden 'crows'. A marvellously colourful bird, the jay is an infrequent garden visitor, preferring the safety of woodlands, but it can sometimes be seen in gardens which are surrounded by mature trees. Its ability to store food in its throat pouch, hamster fashion, enables it to collect food rapidly and put it in a handy hideaway for future consumption. The magpie is the only other member of the crow family you are likely to see regularly, although I have seen jackdaws visiting gardens in different parts of Britain. The magpie is gradually encroaching upon the suburban habitat and is without doubt becoming more common than before. Because of their robust nature, most members of the crow family are able to despatch small birds and mammals with little trouble, a predatory feeding habit which can make them unpopular as they may take fledglings from their nests or nest boxes.

Owls are the predators you are most likely to see in the garden. The

The wren is a retiring bird which feeds on the ground under hedges and shrubs. Unfortunately it does not come to bird tables and it is hard hit by snow, unless it can find food on moss-covered walls or under thick shrubs.

Opposite: The most gaily-coloured birds to visit the garden are the goldfinches which feed almost entirely on the seeds of the dandelion family. Their tiny, tweezer-like bills are used for pulling the seeds from deep in the seed-heads, where other birds cannot reach. The dandelion family includes groundsel, ragwort and the thistles. For this reason, goldfinches are unlikely to visit the best-kept gardens.

tawny owl is the most common bird of prey but, because of its nocturnal habits, is hardly ever actually seen. However, signs of the whereabouts of its roost are long, creamy streaks of droppings near the base of a tree, often a conifer, or regurgitated pellets, made up of the indigestible remains of its meal. During daylight hours owls may be mobbed by other birds and the shrill chatterings and angry calls can lead you to where the harassed bird is attempting to ignore its tormentors. Mobbed owls very rarely retaliate and the taunting birds seem aware of this. At night, however, the roles are dramatically reversed, because tawny owls living in gardens prey upon sparrows, starlings, blackbirds and pigeons. The preponderance of birds in the diet of garden owls contrasts with the mostly mammalian diet of rural ones, which prey upon voles and mice.

The barn owl is the only other bird of prey you are likely to see, mainly because it is less nocturnal in its habits than the tawny owl. It is not a bird of suburban gardens but may nest in derelict buildings such as warehouses or in suburban churches.

One way in which birds can be attracted to the garden is to supply 'artificial' food sources—scraps, leftovers, stale bread and anything else which is rejected for human consumption. (Supplementary feeding is only really necessary during the autumn and winter.) There is no doubt that birds will find this kind of food a useful addition to their diet. If you provide specific foods and perhaps build a bird table, you will certainly encourage a greater variety of birds to your garden.

Readily available, energy-rich foods which always go down well at the bird table are bacon rind, suet, dripping and marrow bones. These should be provided particularly during cold weather. For the seed-eaters, ordinary canary seed, sunflower seeds, flaked maize, corn and peanuts are all readily available from pet shops. If the thought of having to buy food puts you off, try gathering seeds and fruits from outside your garden. They will be a natural source of food for the birds

The magpie gets its name from its black-and-white, pied plumage. Seen at close quarters, the black feathers are shot with shining blues and greens, but this smart appearance does not save the magpie from a poor reputation. It feeds mainly on invertebrate animals but it will rob birds' nests when there is a chance. Magpies are also becoming more common in gardens as they learn to visit bird-tables and steal chicken food.

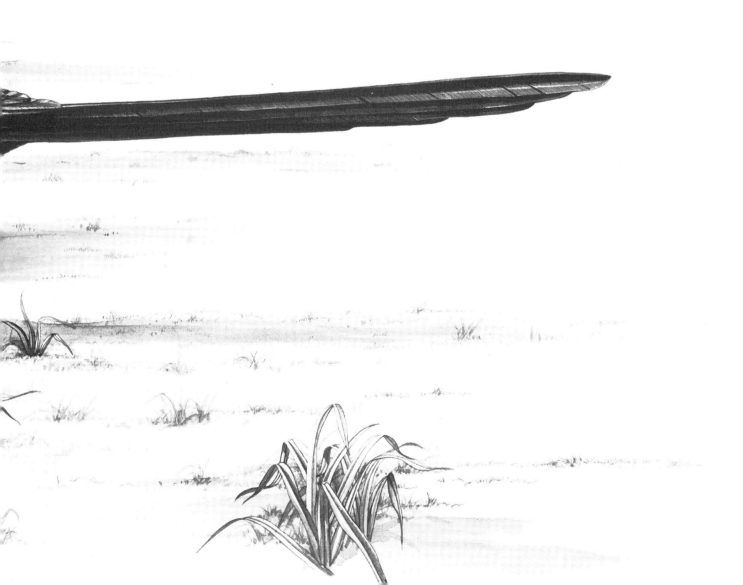

at no cost to you—hazelnuts, horse chestnuts, sweet chestnuts and even the seeds from pine cones can all be used. Fruits such as crab-apples, berries from rowan and holly, and rose hips can be gathered, saved and put to good use later on in winter.

One point that needs stressing is that once you have started feeding garden birds you should never stop suddenly, particularly during a hard winter. Birds will organize their daily routine around the food which is given to them. They expect it and I have heard several reports of birds sitting on ledges and tapping on windows with their beaks, demanding their daily rations. It is unfair to allow them to become reliant upon you and then to let them down when, often, their survival depends on you. Once you have decided to feed them on a regular basis, develop your own routine and the birds will follow it. One feed in the morning and another in the late afternoon will sustain a bird through the day and night. Roosting with a crop full of food ensures that the bird has enough energy to survive a cold night. It cannot be stressed enough that a day without food during hard winter could mean death.

I T IS POSSIBLE to provide more natural food sources at other times of the year. Growing the appropriate plants is a good way of attracting birds. Teasels, thistles, groundsel, sunflowers and Michaelmas daisies, for example, produce seeds and so do scabious, cosmos, evening primroses, antirrhinums and china asters. Some of these plants are considered to be weeds by many gardeners but it is worthwhile allowing them room somewhere in the garden. At the bottom of my own garden I have a large patch of thistles that is left for seed-eaters, and it is regularly visited by goldfinches.

Fruit- and berry-bearing trees and shrubs attract many softbill species. The berries of barberry, blackberry, black or redcurrant, holly, ivy, elder and rowan are enjoyed by a variety of birds. Some, such as elder, are popular with many different species, while othes such as blackcurrant are sought after mainly by thrushes and warblers. Ordinary cultivated fruit trees will appeal to many species and crab-apple is also popular.

Having satisfied the hunger of the seed- and fruit-eaters visiting your garden, it is worth considering the needs of the insectivorous

The bird-table encourages birds to come into the garden. It can be stocked simply with kitchen scraps or elaborate arrangements can be made with peanuts on strings, or in dispensers, and fat in bells. Greedy birds like house sparrows and starlings become unpopular because they finish the food before the shyer and often prettier birds get a chance to eat. Hanging food dispensers give an advantage to the tits—a blue tit is shown approaching and a great tit is hanging on the peanuts. The greenfinch on the bird-table roof likes peanuts suspended in a mesh bag. Some species, like the blackbird, prefer to feed on the ground, so remember to scatter some of the food under the bird-table.

30

birds. Live food, such as maggots and mealworms,
put out on the bird table will be welcomed and
planting vegetation which attracts insects is an indirect
way of feeding them. The more diverse the native plant
species grown in the garden, the greater the variety of insects
and other invertebrates there will be. Butterflies, for example, will
visit many food plants, including buddleia, ice plant, veronica and
nettles. The butterflies and their caterpillars make tasty meals for
many insectivorous birds. Invertebrates which are not encouraged in
gardens but seem always to turn up are snails, slugs and aphids, all of
them splendid fare for many birds, including thrushes and blackbirds.
This means that attracting the right kinds of birds can also help to
control garden pests.

There are two main principles to follow in providing food. First,
supply food mainly during the autumn and winter and at least once a
day. Second, when growing food plants, decide which species you

would like to encourage into the garden and plan the planting with both your needs and the birds' needs in mind.

IN ORDER TO survive and reproduce, a bird has three essential requirements: food, shelter and a nest site. Every bird judges the potential of a habitat on the basis of these three factors, and since these necessities vary from species to species, no one garden will provide all birds with these needs.

Shelter is essential for survival. A few birds shelter by making holes in trees, or finding holes made by other animals, but most roost and shelter in suitable vegetation to protect themselves from the effects of wind and rain.

In the garden, the best shelter can be provided by planting hedges, particularly native species, or constructing fences along the north and east sides. This will reduce the effect of strong winds and driving rain. Privet or hawthorn make a particularly good wind break, and in addition provide nesting and roosting sites and fruits that are a valuable source of food.

When planting with the birds in mind, remember that each species has a preferred height for roosting and nesting. Ideally, therefore, the bird gardener should plant bushes, shrubs and trees of varying heights to give the birds an opportunity to roost or nest at whatever level they require. Bramble bushes or other prickly shrubs, such as barberry, help to deter predators such as cats and make favourite sites for finches and sparrows. The more natural the shelter, the more readily it will be accepted, although some artificial nest boxes may be used for roosting during the winter. The best way of turning an artificial surface, such as a fence or the side of a building, into a potential nest site, is to grow climbing shrubs up it. Ivy or clematis kept thick makes a marvellous roost or nest site for certain birds.

If you plant evergreen bushes you will provide a great bonus for those birds that have to cope with the British winter. Holly, rhododendron or laurel kept fairly bushy and not cut right back, make excellent winter roosts. A bird's choice of roosting site in winter may be critical for its survival. Up to sixteen hours a day is spent roosting. This may seem a lot of time to spend not doing anything but it is essential for a bird to conserve its energy. The only occasion when it really needs to move about in winter is when it is searching for food, but it cannot even afford to waste too much energy doing that.

In winter a bird will live from day to day, desperately trying to eat sufficient food to sustain the heat loss from its body. By sitting on its feet and covering them with its feathers, and by bending its neck under the wing feathers, it can reduce the amount of heat being lost from its body. By fluffing up its feathers it increases the depth of warm air which separates the skin from the cold atmosphere, thereby improving insulation.

The number and variety of birds visiting your garden can be increased by making available suitable nesting sites. Any bird will

A small, well-kept garden may not have the necessary nooks and crevices where birds like to build their nests. This situation can be remedied by putting up nest boxes. They need not be made of the best timber, but it should be sound and solid enough not to warp. Old floorboards are excellent. The boxes should be placed out of reach of cats and sheltered from the hottest sun.

The most common nest box is the 'tit box' with an entrance hole. It is used by tits, nuthatches, tree sparrows and, if the hole is too wide, house sparrows and starlings. An entrance with a diameter of 28 millimetres keeps out the latter birds. The dimensions must allow plenty of room inside: 12 × 12 × 20 centimetres is suitable. When nailing the box together, jointing compound should be used to make the box waterproof, but it is a good idea to leave a drain hole in the bottom.

The open fronted box is easier to make as it does not have to be weatherproofed. It will be used by robins, blackbirds and spotted flycatchers, and should be positioned in cover.

Nest boxes should be put up in autumn so that the birds have plenty of time to explore them before nesting starts in spring. They may even be used for roosting in winter.

have its own fairly fixed idea of what makes a good nest site so you may have to do a little work before you can hope to see it nesting. For example, when you are growing young shrubs, it is best to prune them so that offshoots form forks from the main stem: forks in bushes and trees provide a stable base for nest building. It may be worthwhile going round the garden with a hacksaw or a pair of secateurs, removing stems that could get in the way of the birds. Three or more branches sticking out from a central stem at an angle of approximately 70° make an ideal site for a nest. By inspecting the branch arrangement of trees and bushes carefully, preferably during the time of the year when leaves are absent, you will be able to locate potential nest bases.

Hedges need to be trimmed to the correct dimensions. Something in the region of 1.8 metres (6 feet) high and 0.6 metres (2 feet) thick is about right for many birds. A compact, closely cut hedge will be awkward to find a way in and out of, so it may be necessary to cut away entrances into the hedge to improve access.

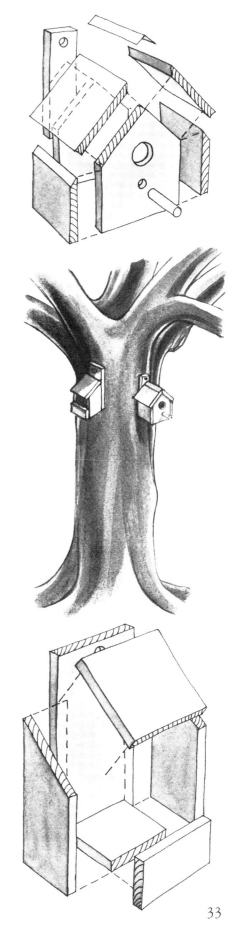

N OT EVERY BIRD nests in bushes and shrubs. Some are hole nesters, preferring the comfort of all-round shelter from the elements and less exposure to predators, and it is not all that easy to meet their needs. If you have old or dying trees in the garden the wood may be soft enough for holes to be made. If there are trees which have to be cut down, leave the stump behind, as this will be a home for invertebrates and may make a good singing post for a thrush or a blackbird, or even a hawking post for a spotted flycatcher.

Undoubtedly, the best provision for hole nesters is a home-made nest box placed in the right position. The dimensions of the box and its design will influence the species likely to use it. A nest box with a small entrance hole of approximately 3 centimetres (1¼ inches) will exclude the larger hole-nesting species such as starlings and sparrows, but allow tits and even nuthatches to get inside.

Not all birds will use a nest box with a single entry hole, preferring one with half of the front open to the outside world. Robins and wrens like an open-fronted nest box when it is hidden away among vegetation and positioned about 1.5 metres (5 feet) from the ground, while pied wagtails and spotted flycatchers prefer a more exposed position.

Nest boxes ought to be put up the autumn before they are needed so that the birds can get used to them. It is always better to put up too many and allow the birds a choice. It is worth emphasizing here that a nest box should be suspended out of reach of cats, on a tree or the side of a building, at a height of between 1.8 metres (6 feet) and 4.5 metres (15 feet). Always shelter the box against the moist west winds and place it facing away from the south so that direct sunlight does not fall on to it.

It is possible to create other forms of nest site in the garden by leaving broken flower pots, piles of bricks and bundles of twigs lying

A bird's parental duties may not end when its young leave the nest. Some birds, like these blue tits, need to be fed while their wing feathers finish growing and they learn how to find their own food. The young birds follow their parents, calling to draw attention to their hunger. After a few weeks, the family gradually disperses.

around in corners. This type of nest is popular with robins, wrens and dunnocks but generally they will only use it when it is situated in a secluded area. A shed door left open may encourage nesting blackbirds, thrushes and swallows to fly inside; if the shed is quiet enough and there is a space somewhere among the debris any one of these species may choose to nest there.

NESTING MATERIALS ARE something else you can provide to persuade birds to stay in your garden. A variety of materials is used during nest construction: mud, dried grass, leaves, feathers, hairs and even spiders' webs. Fill a couple of mesh bags with bits of hay, straw, wool and feathers, suspending one from a tree and fixing one to the ground: this will satisfy the needs of both tree- and ground-dwelling species.

Mud is the main component of the nests of swallows and house martins. During the drought year of 1976, the breeding of these birds was restricted by the lack of mud available for successful nest building. So, if these birds are near you, keep some earth well-watered for their benefit.

Having begged, borrowed and stolen pieces of nesting material, banged your thumb constructing the nest box, scratched yourself reaching that marvellous fork among the brambles, you can now relax and watch your efforts succeed!

Sitting back and not interfering with the birds is certainly the best policy. Most can tolerate only minimal upheaval before they feel so threatened that they desert their nest. So, avoid disturbing them from the time that the adults start building their nests to the time that the baby birds fledge. When the babies grow bigger they may fall out of the nest and hop around the garden. During this period of its life the youngster is vulnerable to a number of dangers. It is fed by the parents and they maintain contact by calling to each other, a situation which continues until the youngster is able to fly.

Many people attempt to hand-rear baby birds and if they are successful, the young bird will have little fear of humans and their pets; letting it go, therefore, may result in it disappearing the way of any other pet food. So, unless you are prepared to accept the responsibility of a pet bird on your hands, leave fledglings alone or, if they seem helpless, put them back into the nest. If you have carried out the many tasks suggested here for the benefit of the birds generally, you have done enough without taking on the responsibility of fostering a baby. Just let Nature take its course. Having a garden enables you to watch the show from the front row.

Mammals and Reptiles

Since earliest times man has hunted his mammal relatives, first with club, spear and arrow, today with horse, hound and gun. Mostly silent and nocturnal, and with sharp senses and dull colouring, these elusive animals tend to avoid us and are usually difficult to see. Even so, a number of them come into close contact with humans, even entering their homes and gardens. We may be quite unaware of their presence, until some sign—a footprint in the snow, or a store of nuts under the garden shed—gives them away.

As in the case of birds and other garden visitors, the locality of a garden and its contents will largely determine which mammals may turn up. The main attractions are food and shelter. Visitors could range from a fox raiding a dust-bin, even inside a town, to a rabbit stealing the cabbages, or a squirrel on the bird table.

In the Scottish Highlands a naturalist managed to invite the pine marten, Britain's rarest mammal, into his garden by putting out food. In Holland there is an interesting account of a roe deer which entered a garden from some neighbouring pine woods to give birth to its tiny kid, and which later became hand-tame. A German naturalist has written of an alarming experience when he woke up one morning to see a wild boar rooting about in his potato patch. It had wandered in from the nearby reserve. Otters have been known to play on lawns which border a river or a lake.

These are somewhat unusual occurrences. Perhaps the commonest of mammal visitors to take up residence in our gardens, whether in town or country, is the hedgehog, an insectivore which should be welcomed as the gardener's friend. It snuffles and snorts around in the undergrowth after dark, searching for earthworms, grubs, snails and eggs, and will even tackle the poisonous adder by using its sharp prickles as a defence. Few enemies, not even most dogs, can harm a rolled-up hedgehog. However, it does face two dangers, from traffic and bonfires. Wandering along roadways and down lanes after dark,

Rarely seen, but often in evidence through heaps of soil on the surface of the ground, the mole is not always popular. Molehills disfigure lawns and the mole's subterranean activities can damage plants in beds. The only consolation is that once a system of tunnels has been excavated, the molehills stop appearing. Only occasionally will a mole appear at the surface to show off its velvet fur and powerful forepaws, set with strong claws and looking like the bucket of a mechanical excavator.

many get run over. As winter approaches it seeks out a place to hibernate, and in a garden this could well be a pile of leaves which then becomes a funeral pyre if it is set alight.

Another insectivore, perhaps not so welcome, is the burrowing mole, which can damage a lawn or disturb flower beds. It may turn up wherever there are earthworms and is active throughout the year; mole casts have even been found pushed up through snow. Occasionally a mole will surface and it is possible to see how well adapted it is for digging. The powerful, curved front feet work like shovels as it 'swims' through the soil. The velvety fur can lie in any direction so as not to become clogged with earth, and the sensitive tail is held upright so that it can judge the width of the tunnels through which it passes. The mole sleeps and breeds in a special chamber within the larger mole-hill or fortress, which is usually covered with turf. A special 'larder' is set aside, containing a store of earthworms which have been bitten to paralyse their movements. When the mole surfaces it may fall victim to birds of prey, especially the tawny owl. Man is its chief enemy.

Shrews, often confused with mice, are also frequent garden visitors. The pygmy shrew is no more than 6 centimetres (2½ inches) long, while its cousin, the common shrew, is about 9 centimetres (3½ inches) long. The white-toothed shrew, which lives in Europe (but not in Britain) has white teeth (hence the name), whereas the other two have their teeth tipped with red enamel. All three do no harm in the garden and are commonly found along hedgerows and among the litter of a woodland floor. Shrews are extremely active little mammals, constantly burning up their energy, and they can eat up to their own

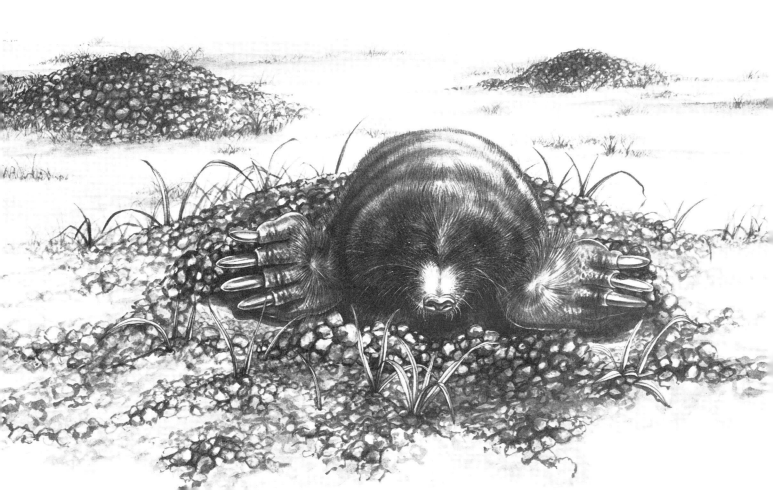

weight in a day. Their pointed, whiskered snouts are continually twitching as they search for insect prey, but they can also tackle animals larger than themselves. A shrew's life is short, little more than eighteen months, and it will quickly die of starvation. Dead bodies are a common sight; death is often due to old age or to cats and other predators. The corpses are discarded because of their musky smell. Night owls are among the shrew's chief enemies.

Shrews keep to regular runways. An interesting experiment showed how they will carefully explore strange surroundings, and return to their nest by the same route. If a stranger appears it is driven off. These tiny mammals appear to be quite fearless of danger, and it is

Shrews are small, insectivorous animals related to the mole and hedgehog. They usually pass unnoticed but their high-pitched squeaks can often be heard. A careful watch may reveal some shrews scurrying through dense ground cover. It would be a great privilege to see a family of shrews 'caravanning'. The babies follow closely behind their mother, each holding the tail of the shrew in front. Caravanning has very rarely been recorded for British shrews.

perhaps as well that they are so small. A curious habit is the way the young follow their parent in a caravan fashion, each gripping the tail of the one in front with its teeth.

Mice, unlike shrews, are rodents, and have curved incisors for nibbling plant food. Shrews have small eyes and ears, and long snouts; mice have large eyes and ears, and blunter snouts. They can, unfortunately, do some damage in gardens, by feeding on vegetables such as peas and beans. The house mouse, which is only too well known and disliked, normally lives in buildings, especially in neglected places, and where there is unprotected food. During summer it moves outdoors, into gardens, fields and hedgerows, and can do harm to the farmer's corn crops. Its coat is a greyish brown, and it has been bred into many varieties as a children's pet.

The house mouse can be confused with the wood mouse, but the latter has larger ears, and is more reddish brown in colour, with greyish underparts and a yellow throat patch. It is nocturnal, and lives in woodland and along hedgerows, although it can also be attracted into country gardens. It searches for seeds, berries and nuts and is such an excellent climber that its store of nuts may sometimes be found in an old bird's nest. It lives and breeds in a tunnel below ground.

The yellow-necked mouse, so called because it has a yellow 'collar' round its throat, is even larger than the wood mouse; it also enters gardens, even houses. Its habits are broadly similar to those of the

wood mouse, although the two normally keep apart. The principal enemies of these mice are weasels, cats and owls.

The tiny harvest mouse is about 6 centimetres (2½ inches) long. This lively little mammal is active by day as well as night, and in summer inhabits cornfields, hedgerows and long grass in open meadows, where it climbs busily among the stalks, using its tail for support. Its characteristic nest, shaped like a tennis ball, is made of grass and corn blades woven around the corn stalks. However, in many areas where modern combine harvesters are in use, this mouse has been driven out of the fields, and its name seems no longer appropriate. During winter it keeps more to underground cover, and to corn ricks. It will also enter gardens in farming country, and may even nest there.

Rats, the larger cousins of mice, are among the most successful colonizers of man's environment, and they, too, will turn up wherever there is undisturbed shelter or unprotected food. The two European species are now almost worldwide, having travelled in ships, caravans and other human transport. They do incalculable harm to food and property, and spread diseases. Of the latter one of the most serious has been the dreaded bubonic plague; caused by a bacillus in the rat-flea carried by the black rat.

Today, due to pest control, the black rat is far less common, and has given way to the more aggressive brown rat. It is, however, still found in isolated pockets, particularly on islands and in buildings situated beside rivers and in dockland. It is the only rat found on ships, from which it is continually introduced into ports. It seldom turns up in gardens, preferring to live under cover, and reports of its presence in gardens are probably due to misidentification, since some black rats are brown, and some brown rats are black. Size and build help to distinguish them: the brown rat is usually larger and more stocky in build, while the black rat is slimmer, with larger ears and a longer tail for its size.

The brown rat, which came originally from northern Asia, can turn

up almost anywhere. It enters gardens, especially where food is carelessly put out for the birds, fed to chickens, or given to pets such as rabbits. It will soon take advantage of such free meals, and may even live in an outbuilding, drain or any nearby tunnel. In towns and villages it lives in sewers, neglected houses and on rubbish dumps. Farms are a special attraction.

Rats have a bad reputation, and are associated with dirt, damage and disease. This is not entirely deserved, as they only exploit man's neglected places and food. Rats born in the wild are very clean. A black rat which I reared from babyhood was an object lesson in personal hygiene, and kept its glossy black fur scrupulously clean. The pet rat is the domesticated form of the brown rat.

VOLES ARE A quite separate family of rodents, recognized by their blunter snouts, small ears and short tails. Some will enter and nest in gardens, and are often brought in the back door as a trophy by the household cat. A common garden resident is the short-tailed or field vole. Yellowish brown in colour, it lives mainly in rough grassland, where it makes a network of runs at ground level and through grass and undergrowth—young forest plantations are especially favoured. The nest of grass is placed at root level. Occasionally, during a so-called population explosion, severe damage is caused by plagues of voles eating young trees and grass. Pastures and sheep walks are said to suffer from vole 'sickness'. The common vole has a darker coat of short hair, and lives more often on cultivated land. It is rarely seen in Britain. The bank vole, more reddish brown in colour, tends to keep to the woods, hedgerows and banksides and makes a burrow for its nest.

If mice, voles and rats are unwelcome in a garden, an exception might be made of the attractive little dormouse, a popular character in story books. Plump in build, covered in rich, chestnut coloured fur and with a hairy tail, this rodent belies its name (from the French *dormir*, to sleep) when it wakes up at night, for it climbs and leaps about in the bushes. It frequents thickets and hedgerows, even parks and gardens, where it builds round nests of grass, leaves and moss, sometimes bound together with strips of honeysuckle bark. Nuts such as hazel and chestnut are its favourite food. It spends the winter in deep hibernation in a nest below ground, curled up in a tight ball. It will sometimes sleep in nest boxes put up for birds.

The common dormouse is the only native species in Britain. At the turn of the century the fat or edible dormouse (so called because of the Roman custom of catching them and fattening them up for banquets) was introduced by Lord Rothschild into his park at Tring in Hertfordshire. One of the few mammals popularly called by its scientific name, *Glis*, it has since spread to the Chiltern Hills where it has acquired the unusual habit of entering and living in buildings and outhouses, especially those where apples are stored. It sometimes damages fruit crops. *Glis* is the largest dormouse, about 20 cen-

The short-tailed vole or field vole is probably the commonest mammal in the countryside and is the main food for many birds of prey and carnivorous mammals. Its main home is in rough grass and it eats mainly grass stems. When particularly abundant, field voles can become a pest.

Voles are immediately distinguished from mice by their tiny eyes, short ears almost hidden in the fur and blunt snout. The field vole has an unmistakably short tail.

timetres (8 inches) in body length and resembles a miniature grey squirrel, with its silvery grey coat and bushy tail.

Intermediate between *Glis* and the common dormouse is the European garden dormouse, which has a greyish upper body and white underparts. It features two dark stripes on its head, and the tail is bushy only at the end. This dormouse is common in orchards and large gardens throughout the country. It nests in bushes and trees, and may use an old bird's nest. The period of hibernation may be spent in a building. Owls appear to be the main enemies of dormice.

IN THE SQUIRREL family, those found in Britain behave somewhat like dormice, but do not hibernate. They are expert tree-climbers, and build nests—dreys—among the branches or in hollows. The American grey squirrel has become firmly established in Britain since it first escaped from a zoo in 1876. It prefers deciduous woodland of oak or beech, and may often be seen in parks and gardens, where it is often hand-tame. At times it can become a nuisance by damaging young trees and in the garden it may attack plants as well as raid the bird table.

The grey squirrel's summer coat contains patches of reddish brown, which may have given rise to a belief that it can interbreed with the

native red squirrel. This never happens. The smaller and much shyer red squirrel has declined in numbers, partly because of the loss of its native conifer woods, but also because of outbreaks of disease. Although the more aggressive grey may occasionally attack it, this is not the main cause of its decline: the grey has merely moved into areas which the red squirrel has left. It is now found mainly in Scotland, Wales, the Lake District and in East Anglia (on Thetford Chase).

The British red squirrel is a separate species from the Continental red squirrel; it has a paler fur, tufted ears and a tail which bleaches almost white during summer. The Continental red is more reddish brown, even black at times. The attractive British red squirrel may enter gardens in areas where there are conifer woods. Its drey is made of bare twigs lined with moss and grass, whereas that of the grey squirrel has twigs with dead leaves attached to them. The squirrel's

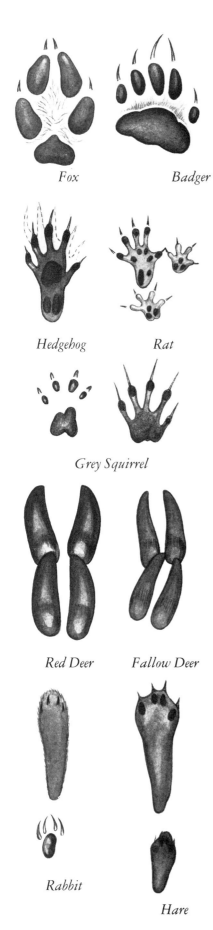

Fox

Badger

Hedgehog

Rat

Grey Squirrel

Red Deer

Fallow Deer

Rabbit

Hare

habit of burying its food is well known, especially during autumn, when fruit and acorns are ripe.

The highly adaptable rabbit is almost too well known to need describing. From its original homeland in south-west Europe, especially Spain, it has spread throughout Europe; it was probably introduced into Britain by the Romans. During Norman times it was regarded as a valuable food and fur animal, and given strict protection in reserves called warrens, but since then it has increased enormously, and is now a serious pest of agriculture and forestry. It can live in almost any territory with workable soil—in mountains, on moorland and sand dunes, in woods, along cliffs and on farmland. It lives in colonies in a system of underground burrows, where the naked, blind young are born, venturing out after dark to feed on a great variety of plants, such as grass, vegetables, farm crops and young trees. Rabbits have caused a marked change of landscape in this country, especially on chalk downland where the close turf and an absence of trees are largely as a result of their feeding habits. On acid soils, they can turn a heather district into grassland. Since the virtual disappearance of rabbits through myxomatosis, many places are now returning to scrub where trees can grow once more.

The myxomatosis virus, from a South American rabbit, was first detected near Paris, then in Kent, and later in Australia. It is spread by a flea and is thought to have been introduced deliberately, which has resulted in much controversy among animal lovers. However, the damage rabbits cause is enormous, and those which enter gardens may not be very welcome. Country gardens suffer most, and vegetables, especially, need protection, as do young trees.

THE BROWN HARE, larger than the rabbit, has reddish fur, with black-tipped ears, and lives above ground. The babies, called leverets, are also born above ground with eyes open, and fully furred. It is a lowland animal which prefers open country on downland, farmland, moorland and dunes. It may enter larger gardens, orchards and vineyards in search of food. Where the rabbit has disappeared the hare may take its place, even in woodland.

During the rut, bucks gather to chase one another and perform aimless mock 'boxing matches'; at this time they are easy to approach, and their antics have earned them the name of 'mad March hares'. A hare is usually flushed from its resting place—the form—at the approach of a human, and sets off at high speed. It keeps to regular routes within its home range, even when coursed by greyhounds.

The smaller blue or mountain hare which, as its name indicates, lives in more mountainous country, is found mainly in the Scottish Highlands, the Pennines and the Peak District of Derbyshire. In the autumn moult its coat turns white. Reports of these hares entering gardens are quite frequent, especially during hard winters when they come down to the more sheltered valleys. A principal enemy is the golden eagle.

44

BATS ARE CREATURES of mystery and darkness, steeped in folklore and legend, but the often feared 'flitter-mouse' is quite harmless, even though a so-called vampire bat does actually exist in tropical America, where it attacks cattle and horses to feed on their blood.

They can hardly be called garden animals, but since they hawk after insects, and shelter in hollow trees and buildings, they frequently appear over gardens at dusk. Some can even be seen well inside towns, in city squares and parks. All European bats are small, and can prove useful to gardeners by hunting for insects.

Bats are the only mammals capable of flight. Their collective name, *Cheiroptera* ('hand-wing'), indicates how the wing is constructed: it is actually a hand with greatly elongated fingers forming a framework over which the skin membrane is stretched. The first digit forms a small hook halfway along each wing, and can be used for climbing and holding on when at rest. Horseshoe bats are named after a curious horseshoe-shaped covering to their faces, called the nose-leaf. When at rest they usually hang upside down from a roof support, in a loft or attic, cave, tunnel or mine-shaft. Both greater and lesser horseshoe bats are largely confined to southern England and Wales. They can tackle large flying beetles and moths, which they eat on the wing or take to a feeding perch. They may occasionally snatch a beetle from the ground.

The more numerous *Vespertilionid*, or typical bats, have more normally shaped faces, and a lobe of skin, the tragus, inside each ear. The nose-leaf and the tragus are believed to assist bats in their remarkable direction-finding ability, called echo-location. Sit in the garden on a warm summer evening and watch how they manage to manoeuvre so skilfully without hitting anything. Pioneer work done in Italy, and later confirmed by experiment in America, has revealed that, apart from making audible squeaks, a bat also emits ultra-sonic notes which bounce off objects and can then be detected as an echo. Echo-location is even used to track down a flying insect.

Commonest and most widespread of the *Vespertilionid* is the little pipistrelle which often frequents built-up areas. It sleeps and hibernates in buildings, hollow trees, behind ivy growing on bark, and wedges itself into tiny cracks. It flies erratically, with many twists and turns, as it hunts insects, mainly gnats. I found one specimen asleep behind some loose bark on a fruit tree in my garden, and it proved a most interesting and instructive pet from which to learn about the strange ways of these little creatures.

The noctule, one of the largest European bats, also frequents areas close to human dwellings, such as parks and gardens. It may appear before dark, and flies rather high, straight and fast, with rapid turns. It is mainly a lowland bat. The scrotine, similar in size and habits, has broader wings, a stouter body and darker fur.

The barbastelle, another woodland bat, has dark fur and ears which meet in the middle of its head. It tends to live a solitary life. Due to

It is often easier to find traces of mammals rather than see them in the flesh. They are shy and do not draw attention to themselves by bright colours like birds, and few make much noise. The presence of mammals in the garden is usually given away by signs where they have been feeding, their droppings and footprints.

Footprints show up well only where there is fine soil and they are frequently difficult to identify because an animal usually puts its hindfeet into the print left by the forefeet. This is called registering. Most tracks will be of cats and dogs and the first step is to learn to distinguish these from wild animals. The illustration shows the tracks of some animals which may come into the garden. They are not drawn to scale.

A fox track is very similar to dog but the toes are closer together and the pad is very small. The claw-marks distinguish dogs and foxes from cats. The badger has a large paw and, like weasels, stoats and otters, it shows five toes. A hedgehog shows five toes on all feet, whereas rats have only four toes on the forefeet. When a squirrel has been bounding, the prints of the hindfeet are placed in front of the forefeet.

Deer are cloven-hoofed, like sheep and goats. The different species are distinguished mainly by the size of the prints. On very soft ground, the small 'dew claws' show behind the hooves.

Rabbits and hares place the hind-feet in front of the forefeet when running fast but not when hopping slowly.

The pipistrelle was once called the flittermouse and is the commonest bat. It is a common sight on fine summer evenings, when it emerges from its roost just after sunset and flies to and fro over gardens or along roads where it can find plenty of flying insects. Small insects are swallowed immediately but larger moths and beetles are carried back to the perch to be eaten at leisure. Prey is detected by echo-location: the bat emits a stream of ultrasonic squeaks, which are pitched outside the range of the human ear, and listens for returning echoes. The bat can be fooled into chasing a pebble tossed in front of it.

Opposite: When a bat is hunting, it emits a series of ultrasonic pulses or clicks and listens for echoes returning from flying insects. The pulses are emitted at frequencies of up to 150,000 Hz. This is well beyond the human limit of hearing of 20,000 Hz. The pulses are extremely loud (and it is a good thing that we cannot hear them) but the returning echoes are very weak. The bats' ears are very sensitive and their echo-location system, which has several features of modern radar equipment, can distinguish between the echoes from insects and those coming from nearby buildings and trees. They can detect a tiny fly from 50 centimetres or more.

the size of its ears, the long-eared bat should be recognizable even in flight; when at rest they are folded back. Flight is a series of glides, and this bat will hover in front of bushes and trees to pick off resting moths and sleeping butterflies from the foliage or tree trunks. Although bats normally sleep during the day, Daubenton's bat, also called the water bat, can often be seen hawking for insects over water in broad daylight and has even been seen to swim.

In contrast to the energetic, short-lived shrews, bats can survive for many years although they spend most of their lives asleep or in hibernation.

We turn from bats, the smallest mammals in this country, to the deer family, which is the largest, and still well represented, in spite of hunting, culling and the loss of native woodlands. The largest member of the family, the red deer, has been hunted since the Stone Age. Most are now found in mountains and on open moorland, having been largely driven from their more natural woodland retreats. But mountains provide poor feeding, so British red deer are now smaller and of poorer physique than those in the forests of Central Europe.

The autumn rut, when stags roar and fight for the hinds, is an impressive sight, and can be witnessed in deer parks as well as in the wild. I have watched it many times in Richmond Park, close to London.

The red deer is indigenous to the continent of Europe and to Britain, but the smaller, fallow deer has been introduced from Asia Minor, mainly for ornament, and to be kept in parks. It is usually an attractive deep fawn in colour, with white spots, but can vary from white to dark brown. The buck has broad, palmate antlers. One or two almost black herds, such as the one in Epping Forest, once a royal hunting forest, were imported purely for sport.

The only other native European deer is the small roe, about the size of a large dog. The buck has forked and pointed, upright antlers. Roe deer prefer open woodland with plenty of undergrowth in young plantations, in which they can hide unnoticed. Red and fallow deer live in herds but the roes congregate in families. During the rut in midsummer the buck will chase his doe, often in a circle around a bush or tree. The chase wears a footpath, called a deer ring.

The remaining deer are importations, and have mainly escaped from zoos or game parks. One of them, the tiny muntjak or barking deer, only 50 centimetres (20 inches) high, is now firmly established in parts of England. The buck has short, simple antlers on a long and hairy base, called the pedicel, and a sharp, dog-like call. I know of at least one large garden where the owner has managed to encourage these deer to enter and feed. The Chinese water deer has also settled in parts of England. The buck has no antlers but has long tusks—the canines—in the upper jaw, and can be recognized by its distinctive hump-shaped body outline and its whistling call.

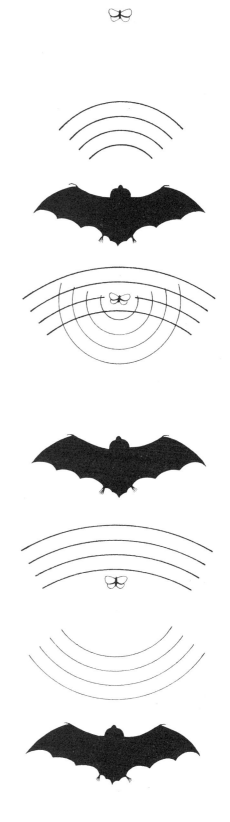

CARNIVOROUS MAMMALS which hunt live prey do not, on the whole, enter gardens unless suitable food is available. Those most likely to turn up are one or other of the members of the weasel family. Mostly they have slender bodies on short legs, bodies built for getting into holes and burrows in search of prey. The family name of *Mustelidae* refers to the powerful scent, sometimes highly nauseating, which is emitted from the glands at the base of the tail, and which serves both as a means of communication and as a line of defence. Weasels have traditionally been persecuted by man, as well as being trapped for their valuable fur; many are now bred on special 'fur farms'.

The smallest of the family is the tiny weasel, about 20 centimetres (8 inches) in length, which feeds on mice and voles. The larger stoat (known as the ermine), recognizable by the permanent black tip to its tail in all seasons, turns white during winter in northern areas. It can tackle prey larger than itself, such as rabbits, game birds and poultry. Both species are very inquisitive, and will come out of hiding and stand up on their hind legs to look at a passer-by.

The less common polecat is now confined to central Wales, usually on farmland, and often near dwellings. It has a dark coat and a 'mask' of black and white on its face. The albino ferret is a domesticated polecat used for driving rabbits out of burrows by gamekeepers and farmers—and poachers! It can easily be seen after dark. (There is also a dark coloured hybrid, the polecat-ferret.) One day a young ferret, apparently lost, wandered into our London garden and was kept as a most gentle and playful pet. In spite of its reputation for having a foul stench (its old name of foumart means 'foul marten'), this one never once disgraced itself.

THE BEAUTIFUL PINE marten, or sweet-mart, is even less numerous, because it has been so much persecuted for the sake of its rich fur, and driven into more remote areas, mainly coniferous forests in the Scottish Highlands. It has a chestnut coloured fur with a creamy white patch on the throat; the smaller European beech marten, which is not usually found in Britain, has a white throat patch divided into two halves. It is less dependent on woodland and often turns up in the neighbourhood of houses. It may even go right into villages and the outskirts of towns as, indeed, will the red fox.

This wily member of the dog family manages to hold its own, in spite of hunting and trapping. Its entry into built-up areas may be due to the loss of its chief prey, the rabbit, which became scarce after myxomatosis. The sharp yap of the dog fox, and the scream of the vixen during the mating season, are common sounds at night. In my present garden fox tracks are often to be seen during snowfalls. There are still rabbits in the neighbourhood and a neighbour's chicken house is sometimes raided—a hungry vixen will even attack and kill a cat for food.

The vixen, a somewhat lazy mother, will make use of an existing hole by enlarging a rabbit burrow, or may occupy part of a badger sett. On occasions, when badger-watching, it is possible to see fox cubs emerge from one end of the sett and badger cubs from the other. An

occupied fox den can be recognized by the musty smell and the scattered remains of meals at the entrance.

In contrast to the fox, the badger, a large, digging weasel (*bécheur* is the French word for digger), is clean and house-proud. It constantly cleans out the entrance to the sett and carries in fresh bedding of grass, straw or bracken to line its nesting chamber. Unlike the fox it never fouls its home, but uses a latrine area close by, where it digs small pits for lavatories. In some places, where buildings have encroached on an occupied sett, the badgers have been reluctant to move, even though surrounded by houses.

Both fox and badger will occupy and rear their families in larger gardens, if allowed to do so. Many a tolerant owner has had the pleasure of gaining their confidence, even managing to feed the cubs by hand. There is a well-known example of human cooperation with foxes in a south London suburb, where foxes breed regularly along the embankment of a railway line. Commuters on their way to work can see them sitting by the line, watching the trains go by. Neighbouring gardeners feed them, and they have even been filmed.

Pond Life

A pond can make any garden more attractive, particularly if it becomes a main feature, and it can also greatly increase the diversity of wildlife. Birds will visit the pond to drink and bathe; many varieties of insects may come to lay their eggs in the water; amphibians, such as frogs, toads and newts, may breed in the pond, and live in or near it. All these animals benefit from the pond's presence and it also provides you, the wildlife gardener, with a whole new habitat to consider.

Having built a pond, you can sit back and wait for colonization to take place. Many micro-organisms will be transported to the pond as wind-blown spores or eggs—sometimes eggs are carried on the feet of birds which visit to drink or bathe. Adult insects may carry various spores on their bodies and they will, of course, introduce their own eggs into the pond, which will then become insect larvae.

It does not take long for the pond to start buzzing with life. Green algae, primitive and advanced plants soon start to grow. Fish, such as sticklebacks, may suddenly arrive, transported as eggs. Eventually a community establishes itself. It is possible to help it along by adding plants, snails, mud from other ponds and fish bought from aquarists. It is important not to introduce too much of anything, as an excess of any one species can upset the natural balance.

The forms of life occupying a pond community will vary depending on many factors, some physical—such as the chemical composition of the water—others biological, such as the local distribution of a particular species. The actual size of the pond may itself influence the diversity of organisms living in it: larger ponds may attract more organisms.

We shall be considering here mainly the more common forms of invertebrate life that are found in a garden pond. They can be divided into two main categories: first, those organisms which live in the pond but breathe air; and second, those that are completely aquatic and breathe in water. Amphibians and reptiles are dealt with separately.

In the first category are those animals that live under water but must come to the surface to breathe air; they are sometimes called partially aquatic animals. Because they come to the surface regularly they are more conspicuous to the careful observer than the animals which lurk in the depths of the pond.

Some beetle species can be included in this category. All pond-dwelling beetles are capable of flying out of the water, changing from

Nothing increases the diversity of wildlife in a garden more than a pond. It is a drinking place for birds and mammals, and attracts many water insects. The first to arrive will probably be the pond skaters (centre) and the whirligig beetles (bottom left) next to them, which can fly in. Mayflies (centre right) visit to lay their eggs and their nymphs will be found later underwater. The wriggling larvae of gnats (top) provide food for larger animals, like the crested newt (bottom right). Stocking the pond with wild water plants improves its appearance and makes it more attractive to animals.

50

an aquatic life-style to an aerial one. Some may do this in search of new feeding or breeding grounds and, as a consequence, the number occupying your pond may fluctuate considerably.

Hydrobius is a small vegetarian beetle which has stiff, hairlike structures on its underside. These trap air collected from the surface and give the beetle a silvery appearance. A summer visitor to your pond may be the whirligig beetle, which collects in large numbers and gyrates in circles on the surface of the pond, hence its name. The great diving beetle is large and robust, and highly carnivorous. If you value your pond goldfish, make every effort to discourage this beetle as it is quite capable of attacking prey larger than itself—and that includes any interfering fingers!

Another group of insects known as water bugs may pay a visit to your pond. Underwater varieties include the water boatman, and the lesser water boatman. The former is the larger of the two and is immediately recognizable as it has a tendency to swim upside down. The lesser water boatman has a much less pointed body and swims with its back uppermost. Both swim well, aided in part by their long, oar-like hind legs. Their movement through the water is rather jerky.

Both types are common in ponds. The larger water boatman sticks its back end out of the water to collect air, which is retained as a glistening film that forms on the animal's under side. Having thus become quite buoyant, the animal then has to struggle down into the watery depths and, when not moving, it must cling on to something

to counteract a tendency to float to the surface. It is very carnivorous but the lesser water boatman is herbivorous, sucking up the detritus from the pond bed.

Another water bug that might find its way into your pond is *Nepa*, the water scorpion, so-called because the first pair of legs is modified for grabbing prey and looks rather like a scorpion's 'pincers'. The other similarity lies in its sting, a long siphon situated at the end of the animal's abdomen which is used for breathing. The siphon is pushed up through the water's surface when the animal needs to breathe. The body is flat and the fore-wings conceal a pair of bright red hind-wings, which contrast with its overall dark colour. In spite of these wings, the water scorpion is unable to fly.

Among bugs, there is one which will almost certainly visit the pond. It is an air-breathing surface dweller, never living underneath the water but always on top, skating on the surface film, and called, appropriately enough, the pond skater, *Gerris*. It is long and thin with splayed-out legs which prevents it from sinking below the surface. It is carnivorous, chasing after any insects that get stranded on the surface of the water.

AMONG THE PARTIALLY aquatic animals are certain types of air-breathing snails. The two most common species are the great pond snail, *Limnaea stagnalis*, and the wandering snail, *Limnaea pereger*. Although they both belong to the same genus they are easy to tell apart: the former is large with a hefty shell that has a long spire; the latter is noticeably smaller and its shell is stubby with a short spire, the first whorl forming most of the whole shell.

Other snails which may choose to take up residence in your pond are the ramshorn snails, belonging to the genus *Planorbis*. These are noticeably different from the *Limnaea* snails because they have a shell which, looked at from the side, resembles a slice of Swiss roll.

Sometimes snail's eggs are carried to the pond on the feet of birds visiting the water for a bath or a drink. If no snails manage to reach your pond, it is worth getting some.

Once the snails have settled down they will start to produce large gelatinous egg masses, like transparent toothpaste, in which there are black or white dots. These masses can be seen stuck to the sides of the pond, or found among water weed. The breeding should be encouraged as young snails provide food for some of the carnivorous pond residents.

The last group of partially aquatic animals is insect larvae. Some species are noticeably more abundant than others, particularly the small gnat and midge larvae, easily recognizable as long, thin, segmented animals with tiny hair-like structures and appendages decorating parts of the body. The next stage in the metamorphosis of gnat larvae is the pupal stage. Each pupa has a large swelling on the front end, which looks almost like an outsized head. In this swelling exists the developing adult insect.

The simplest garden pond is made by lining a hole with thick polythene. Steps at two depths make it suitable for different kinds of plants. The pond should be at least 40 centimetres deep and sloping sides reduce the danger of caving in. A foundation of sand, newspapers or old sacks will protect the polythene lining from being punctured on sharp stones.

When the polythene has been laid, fill the pond so that it takes on its final shape, then trim it so that there is about a 10 centimetre overlap. This should be buried under a border of paving or turf, both to make the pond look better and to prevent the polythene from perishing in the sunlight.

The final stage is to add waterplants. Some are free-floating but rooted varieties need to be planted in flowerpots or other containers so that they can be lifted easily when the pond is cleaned. A cover of small-mesh wire netting is useful for trapping dead leaves when they fall in autumn, and grass-cuttings when the lawn is mown.

The pond should have steps or a ramp so that young amphibians, or hedgehogs and mice which have fallen in, can climb out and so that small birds can drink or bathe.

Many other insects lay their eggs in ponds and produce remarkable-looking larvae. The rat-tailed maggot is the larva of a species of dronefly. Generally resembling a maggot in its overall appearance, it has a long breathing siphon at its posterior end.

The larvae of beetles have segmented bodies, three pairs of legs, a well-defined head, often armed with a pair of fearsome jaws and at the posterior end, filamentous appendages. The larva of the great diving beetle is highly carnivorous, preying on other insects, tadpoles and small fish.

The larvae of caddis flies are often surrounded by a protective cylindrical case, constructed from bits of plant material or gravel glued together. The kind and size of particles used for case construction varies from species to species, though not all caddis larvae build cases.

Two of the more common pond species are *Triaenodes* and *Phryganea*. Both build rather neat cases of plant material cut into small rectangles and arranged in a spiral. *Phryganea* builds a long, heavy case while that of *Triaenodes* is lighter, and tapers to a point. Both are omnivorous.

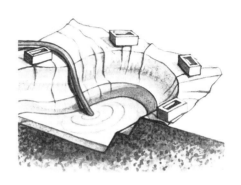

Other insects, such as mayfly and dragonfly, spend part of their life cycle in ponds as nymphs. They have mechanisms for breathing oxygen from water and are therefore aquatic. With this type of insect development there is no change to a pupal stage: the nymph continues growing by shedding its skin until it reaches the last stage, when it is ready to break out of its nymphal skin and emerge as an adult.

A mayfly nymph is easily recognized by its segmented body with well-defined head, thorax and abdomen. The head carries a pair of compound eyes and antennae, the thorax three pairs of legs and at least one pair of larval wings. The abdomen is the most characteristic part of the body, possessing a series of flap-like structures running down each side. These flaps are the nymph's gills and enable it to extract oxygen from the water. At the end of the abdomen are three feathery bristles known as the anal cerci.

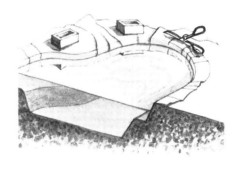

The nymph of a dragonfly is very similar, except that it is larger and lacks external, flap-like gills. It has gills lining its rectum, and water is pumped in and out to supply the gills with oxygen.

Dragonfly nymphs have a mechanism known as a mask for seizing their prey. The mask is folded under the head and ends in a pair of jaws. When prey passes in front of the nymph, the mask is rapidly extended forward to grab it and take it to the mouth for consumption.

If your garden pond attracts adult dragonflies or damselflies you will be treated to a spectacular array of colours and a marvellous sight, particularly if they are courting and mating.

The next category is the completely aquatic animal which never breathes air and remains under water all the time. Many of them are minute. One such animal is the water flea, *Daphnia*, not a flea but a crustacean related to crabs and lobsters. *Daphnia* may be familiar as the live food that can be bought from aquarists for feeding to aquarium fish. Although it is so tiny, it can be seen with the naked eye, swimming in a jerky manner.

Right: Dragonflies visit ponds to hunt the smaller insects which gather there, and they must stay to court and lay their eggs. The eggs are either shed into the water or laid in the stems of plants. They hatch into nymphs which are carnivorous like their parents. Eventually, the nymphs climb up a water plant, the skin splits and adult dragonflies emerge.

Vast numbers of water fleas may be found in the pond during summer, because they reproduce parthenogenetically—that is, without mating with a male. There are various other small crustaceans which inhabit the pond and these, together with the water flea, form the food of many larger animals which live there.

Another crustacean, *Asellus*, the water-louse, is much larger, growing up to 2 centimetres (¾ inch) long. It looks something like a flattened wood-louse and is common in water systems throughout Great Britain. Do not confuse it with *Gammarus*, the freshwater shrimp, which swims on its side and is flattened from side to side, not from top to bottom like the water-louse. *Gammarus* tends to prefer fast-running water but may sometimes be found living quite happily in a garden pond.

OTHER CREATURES which may be seen from time to time include flatworms, leeches and worms. The flatworms are tiny, flat, dark symmetrical strips which glide over surfaces at a steady rate. They are best looked at in a jam jar where it is possible to watch them slithering over the glass sides. Flatworms are predators, feeding on other small animals in the pond. Each one possesses a tube-like structure called the pharynx, through which it sucks up the body juices of its prey.

Leeches are fairly easy to recognize being long, thin, wormlike animals which have a sucker at both ends of the body. They can sometimes be seen swimming in a sinuous way through the water or attached to a rock by one sucker and waving the body about, giving an impression of indecisiveness! Not all leeches are blood-suckers. The species that live in the garden pond tend to be the ones that feed on worms, crustaceans and snails. Only one type, the rare medicinal leech, sucks human blood.

Overleaf: A scene of activity under the pond's surface. A pair of great diving beetles swim down from the surface. The male on the right has pads on its forelegs, which he uses to grasp the female in mating. These beetles are carnivorous, as are two bugs, the water scorpion (left) and the backswimmer (top). The lesser waterboatman (bottom right) is a plant-eating bug. Above is a giant pond snail, another plant eater, and below are two hydras whose tentacles capture tiny animals. The leeches hanging by their suckers to water plants cannot harm human beings; they attack much smaller victims. The caddis nymph (bottom right) is protected by a case which it has made from pebbles. It will eventually turn into a moth-like adult. The comma-shaped animals hanging from the surface are pupae from which mosquitoes will emerge. The tubifex worms (bottom left) come out of their burrows and wave their bodies to breathe.

Worms are relatives of leeches. Most pond-dwelling worms resemble the ordinary earthworm in appearance, and it is extremely difficult to tell the different species apart. One type which stands out is the worm *Tubifex*, which lives within a tube. *Tubifex* worms can be seen living together in the mud at the bottom of the pond, each waving the projecting posterior part of its body from side to side in order to collect together suspended particles of matter on which it then feeds.

Other completely aquatic organisms which may be seen from time to time in the garden pond are *Hydra*—water mites—and certain species of snail. *Hydra*, related to jellyfish and sea anemones, is basically a long stalk with tentacles to catch various prey animals. It is the nearest thing to a freshwater sea anemone. Water mites are fairly distinct, being brightly coloured. They are generally about a couple of millimetres long and are carnivorous.

Finally, there may be one or two completely aquatic snails living in the garden pond. The horny orb shell, for example, is a pea-sized mollusc, normally light in colour. It has two shells which fit together in the same way as the shells of a mussel. The lake limpet may be

54

found attached to the leaves of water weeds on which it feeds. It is rather like a miniature, flattened limpet and is dark in colour.

Plants are an essential part of any aquatic community and every pond must have a selection. They provide oxygen from photosynthesis and also food and shelter for many pond organisms. The more primitive plants, such as algae, will find their own way to the pond. They may sometimes produce strange effects, particularly during summer: high temperatures speed up the rate of reproduction and lead to blooms, when the single-celled algae turn the water into something resembling pea soup.

Filamentous algae, such as *Spirogyra*, mass together and form floating mats which can completely cover the water surface. It is best to remove most of them as quickly as possible.

The only plants that need concern us here are the submerged and floating varieties and one or two emergent plants that can be used to decorate the edges of the pond.

Many different submerged plants may be bought from aquarists. Perhaps the most suitable are Canadian pondweed, water milfoil, hornwort and water crowfoot. With the exception, perhaps, of hornwort, these plants should be anchored in the substrate of the pond so that they can take root. Canadian pondweed may be left to float if need be. Water crowfoot produces attractive flowers during early summer.

Floating plants, such as duckweed and frogbit, do not root in the pond bed but float on the surface, their leaves spreading out over a wide area. Make sure that these plants do not smother the surface as this stops sunlight from getting into the pond.

Plants such as arrowhead and various water lilies can be planted in baskets and then placed along the edges of the pond, submerged in the shallows. Plant water lilies only where there is adequate space for them to grow.

Garden ponds now make a significant contribution to wildlife conservation through their role as breeding sites for some of Britain's amphibians—frogs, toads and newts. In the past they could rely on village ponds, cattle ponds and old ditches, but today many of these spawning sites have been lost through drainage of agricultural land, new highway construction and land-fill. The numbers of common frogs have fallen dramatically in recent years,

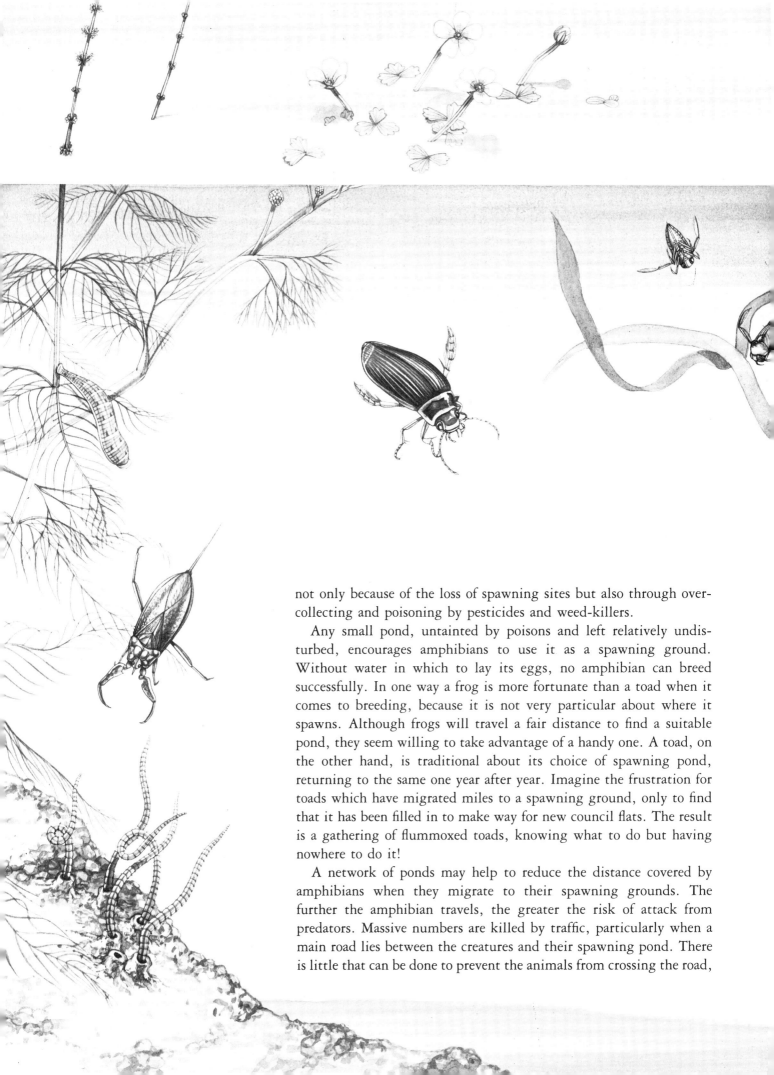

not only because of the loss of spawning sites but also through over-collecting and poisoning by pesticides and weed-killers.

Any small pond, untainted by poisons and left relatively undisturbed, encourages amphibians to use it as a spawning ground. Without water in which to lay its eggs, no amphibian can breed successfully. In one way a frog is more fortunate than a toad when it comes to breeding, because it is not very particular about where it spawns. Although frogs will travel a fair distance to find a suitable pond, they seem willing to take advantage of a handy one. A toad, on the other hand, is traditional about its choice of spawning pond, returning to the same one year after year. Imagine the frustration for toads which have migrated miles to a spawning ground, only to find that it has been filled in to make way for new council flats. The result is a gathering of flummoxed toads, knowing what to do but having nowhere to do it!

A network of ponds may help to reduce the distance covered by amphibians when they migrate to their spawning grounds. The further the amphibian travels, the greater the risk of attack from predators. Massive numbers are killed by traffic, particularly when a main road lies between the creatures and their spawning pond. There is little that can be done to prevent the animals from crossing the road,

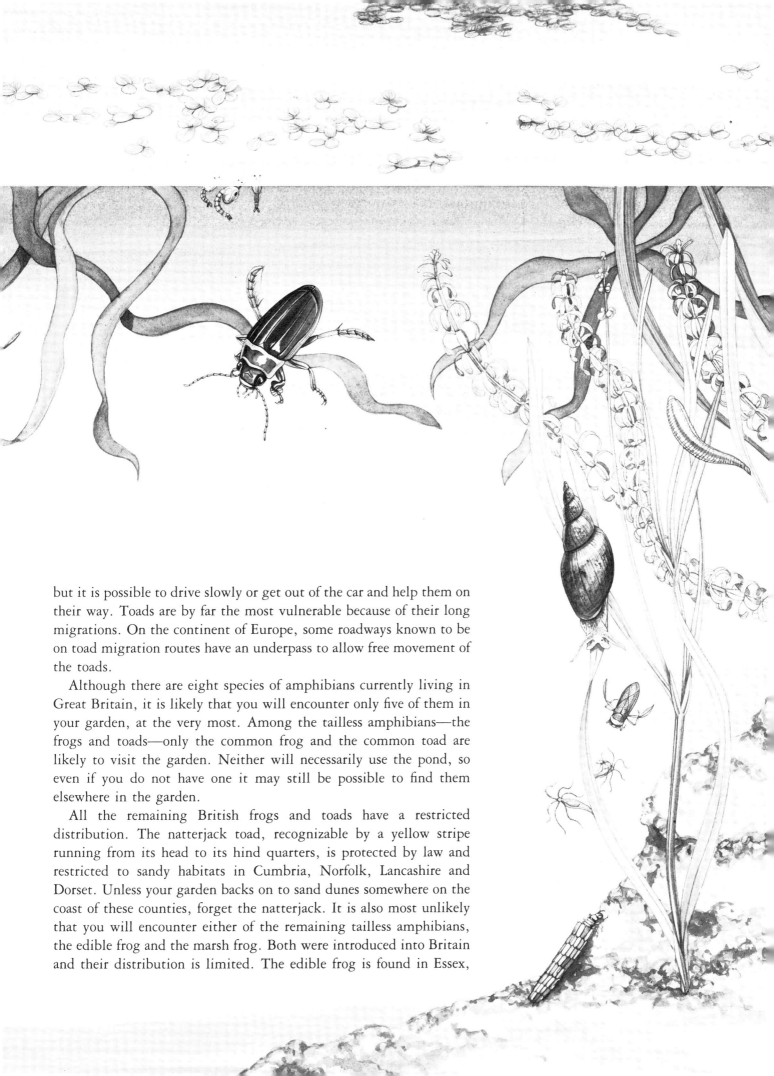

but it is possible to drive slowly or get out of the car and help them on their way. Toads are by far the most vulnerable because of their long migrations. On the continent of Europe, some roadways known to be on toad migration routes have an underpass to allow free movement of the toads.

Although there are eight species of amphibians currently living in Great Britain, it is likely that you will encounter only five of them in your garden, at the very most. Among the tailless amphibians—the frogs and toads—only the common frog and the common toad are likely to visit the garden. Neither will necessarily use the pond, so even if you do not have one it may still be possible to find them elsewhere in the garden.

All the remaining British frogs and toads have a restricted distribution. The natterjack toad, recognizable by a yellow stripe running from its head to its hind quarters, is protected by law and restricted to sandy habitats in Cumbria, Norfolk, Lancashire and Dorset. Unless your garden backs on to sand dunes somewhere on the coast of these counties, forget the natterjack. It is also most unlikely that you will encounter either of the remaining tailless amphibians, the edible frog and the marsh frog. Both were introduced into Britain and their distribution is limited. The edible frog is found in Essex,

Middlesex, Surrey and Kent, the marsh frog almost exclusively in the Romney Marshes in Kent. Neither species has extended its range very far since its introduction and neither occupies gardens to any major extent.

The remaining amphibians are three species of newt: the smooth newt, the palmate newt and the warty newt. In principle, it is possible to find any one of these species or all three in the garden.

Because of their overall similarity in appearance, it is worth

mentioning the ways of distinguishing between them. The warty newt is rather different from the other two, being dark on the back and orange on the belly, with dark blotches on both. The skin is quite coarse. During the breeding season the male grows a high, spiky, dorsal crest, which is indented at the base of the tail. This species tends to be more aquatic than the others and may remain in a pond all the year round.

The most widespread newt in Britain is the common, or smooth, newt, as it is sometimes known. This species readily inhabits gardens and out of the breeding season it may be found under stones, leaf litter, old rotting logs or in similar damp places.

The common newt, particularly the female, can easily be confused with the palmate newt. Its overall colour is olive or brown, but it also has blotches on its throat, a feature lacking in the palmate newt. These blotches are apparent on the belly, too, and so is a red or orange central stripe running down the belly. The skin is smooth. The breeding male has a high, undulating crest running from its neck to its tail and also prominent dark blotches all over the body.

The palmate newt is the smallest of the three species. Another smooth-skinned newt, it resembles the common newt in colour and appearance, even to the coloured stripe running down the belly. There may, however, be a dark stripe at the side of the head and the underside may be devoid of spots. Breeding males have a low, smooth crest on the back which becomes slightly higher on the tail. This ends in a filament and the hind feet are noticeably webbed. This newt will readily breed in clear, shallow water and has been known to spawn in puddles.

The common frog catches insects and other small animals with its long tongue. They have to be moving, otherwise it does not notice them. The garden is becoming an increasingly important home for frogs and other amphibians because the countryside is losing its ponds and wet places. The amphibians lay their spawn in garden ponds and spend the rest of the year in quiet undisturbed corners of gardens where there is plenty of cover.

THE GARDEN ITSELF, then, can provide a terrestrial habitat for amphibians but during the breeding season it is the pond that becomes the focus of attention for them. Generally speaking, the urge to breed comes about after the amphibians have completed their hibernation and wake up for spring. Frogs and toads begin breeding in mid-March or late April. Both males and females migrate to a body of water where they court and spawn. Once the eggs are fertilized by the male, they are left on their own to develop. No parental care is shown, except perhaps for choosing the best place to lay eggs in the case of some newt species.

In frogs and toads, fertilization is external, the male releasing his sperms into the water after the female has extruded her eggs. Toad spawn can be found wrapped around water weed in the deeper parts of a pond. Frogs prefer to spawn in shallower water, and as a consequence they are more likely to use a garden pond.

Once the eggs have been fertilized, metamorphosis may vary from 65 to 108 days for the toad, depending on local weather conditions: the warmer it is, the quicker the metamorphosis.

Frog metamorphosis is a standard textbook story so need be mentioned only briefly here. When the frog larva or tadpole first hatches from the egg, it is a small black blob with a tail and external gills near the head. About three weeks after hatching the gills disappear, and by eight weeks the hind legs are fully formed. By twelve weeks both the front legs are through. Later on, the tail is reabsorbed and the baby frog is ready to move on to land. The beginning of June is the time when froglets start to make their move and, at this time, even if you do not have a pond, they will start to appear in the garden.

My own garden seems to be popular with frogs. There is an overgrown section at the bottom, with thistles and brambles, and patches of weed in between rows of cultivated vegetables. This part of the garden, and the long grass at the edge of the lawn, is their haven. It provides food, in the form of the many invertebrate species which occupy the diverse habitats, and there is shelter to be found among the weeds and tangled shrubs. On several occasions I have counted eight or nine frogs in the space of a few minutes, in different parts of the garden.

By early October there are no more frogs to be seen. It is about this time that the frog finds a suitable place for hibernation—a cavity or, preferably, somewhere in or near water. It is doubtful whether adult frogs will use the pond in which they breed for hibernation, although over-wintering froglets will bury themselves in mud at the bottom of the pond in which they hatched. When a frog hibernates, the body metabolism slows down and the demand for oxygen is drastically reduced. While in the pond, a hibernating frog may obtain oxygen from the water via its skin which is thin and damp enough to allow oxygen through it; there is no need for it to come to the surface to breathe.

Garden frogs may, like their more rural relatives, migrate to suitable hibernating areas. Toads, on the other hand, often remain in the garden, hibernating under piles of stones or wood. Sometimes toads find their way into cellars and sheds where they spend the winter in hibernation. In early spring, toads and frogs migrate to their spawning waters.

THE COURTSHIP AND breeding of newts is rather different and their courtship behaviour is much more romantic than that of frogs and toads. The male newt grows a colourful breeding dress, guaranteed to attract even the most unreceptive female. Having caught the attention of a female newt, the flamboyant male proceeds to seduce her with nudges of his nose against her body, at the same time waving his tail and revealing his bright colours. By remaining, the female accepts the male and he responds by depositing a spermatophore—an elongated packet of sperms—upon the pond-bed, which the female then takes up into her body. Once the sperms have fertilized the eggs, she lays the eggs individually and very carefully wraps each one up in water weed for protection.

The newt tadpole is a miniature adult except that it has external gills which become more feathery as it grows. In the sixth week its front limbs appear, followed in the eighth week by the hind limbs. Four to five months is needed for metamorphosis to take place. Sometimes eggs laid late in the year produce tadpoles which have to over-winter. These complete their metamorphosis in May or June of the following year.

Newts tend to stay around a breeding pond for most of the year, settling down in one area and remaining there, provided that the

habitat meets their needs. The over-wintering period can be a dangerous time for them. It is advisable, therefore, for the garden owner to provide suitable hibernation areas to ensure that they are still there next year to grace the pond and garden. Favoured spots are under stones, logs or piles of leaves. Like toads, newts will also use sheds and cellars for hibernation.

Amphibians in the garden always arouse great interest and many people are surprised that frogs will happily occupy suburban gardens, even those only a few miles from the centre of London. Provided that conditions are suitable and that there is a reasonable pond available for breeding, they seem very willing to make use of even the most modest facilities that people provide.

Amphibians, unlike some mammal, bird or insect species, can never be regarded as pests, even in the most cultivated garden, and should always be encouraged. Although never as easy to watch as other garden animals, such as birds or butterflies, they are as fascinating in their own way and, unlike these other forms of life, tend to remain in the garden year after year.

Of the reptiles and amphibians, it is the latter which can be most commonly found using the garden as a habitat. Reptiles tend to use gardens infrequently and, when they do, it is normally a rural garden. Out of the six species of British reptiles, only two can be considered as garden dwellers, and both of these are lizards. The likelihood of finding any species of snake in a garden is very remote.

The six species of reptiles include three snakes: the adder, probably the commonest snake in Britain and the only venomous species, the harmless grass snake, and the smooth snake, a very rare type confined to a few areas in the south of England and protected by law.

Lizards include the sand lizard, another rare reptile protected by law, the common lizard and the slow-worm, which is legless. The last two species are found in most counties of Britain but unlike the common lizard, the slow-worm has never reached Ireland.

The common lizard is generally a brown colour, although there may be hints of olive or grey in some specimens. It seems to require a humid environment and avoids habitats which are too hot. Like most other lizards, it enjoys basking in the sun: it will even climb walls to reach a favourite basking spot.

The habitats in which it is found range from sand dunes through wasteland and open woods to heaths and bogs. Obviously, many gardens provide a suitable habitat but that does not guarantee that it will live there. Probably common lizards will only enter gardens which are within or on the outskirts of a local colony. For example, I found common lizards on Wimbledon Common and undoubtedly the species also occupied the gardens on the perimeter of the Common. But very few suburban gardens are occupied by this lizard.

THE SLOW-WORM, although a lizard, has no legs and in the eyes of many people immediately falls into the category of a snake. It therefore tends to be treated with the same innate dread that human beings often have, unjustifiably in most cases, of snakes. The slow-worm can readily be distinguished from any snake by its smaller, thinner body, its more lizard-like head, the fact that it has eyelids and can blink (something which no snake can do), and also by its brown skin, which appears smooth and polished. They should be encouraged to live in the garden because slugs are their favourite food.

Like the common lizard, the slow-worm is found in a variety of habitats and is abundant in certain parts of the south and west of England. Apart from basking in the sun, it is rarely seen in daylight, preferring to remain hidden under rocks, logs and leaves. It makes its appearance in the evening or after rain, but can sometimes be encountered by lifting up flat stones or even sheets of corrugated iron. By nature the slow-worm is a burrower and in loose soil will bury its body, leaving just the head protruding. It rarely bites but it may struggle, and it is remarkable how strong its body feels when it writhes between your fingers. Both this lizard and the common lizard have to be handled carefully as either may drop its tail in response to being grabbed. This is a normal method of self-defence in many lizards—and so is voiding the contents of the bowels all over your hand! Slow-worms hibernate in October and use piles of leaves or heaps of stones; some have even been found hibernating in walls. The common lizard also hibernates in October.

If reptiles are living in your garden, you are extremely fortunate in being able to witness the life-style of these animals at close quarters.

Butterflies and Moths

Butterflies and moths, known to entomologists as the *Lepidoptera*, are the most attractive of insects. Butterflies especially can be as much an adornment to a garden as the flowers upon which the average gardener lavishes so much care and attention. Without needing to do anything at all about it, you will be favoured with visits from a remarkable range of species, even in the heart of a large town or city. For a little extra trouble, the number and variety of visiting butterflies and moths can be increased considerably. If you live on the outskirts of a town or in a country village you can, if you wish—and especially if you have enough acreage—turn your garden into a real sanctuary for these insects. Surely, nobody would deny that the beauty of a garden's flowers is greatly enhanced by the sight of small tortoiseshells, peacocks, red admirals and other gorgeous butterflies, sucking their nectar?

To put this in numerical terms, in the average suburban garden, at some time or other, one can expect to see fifteen or more species of butterflies, plus 150 or more different species of moths. Even an urban garden in a large city such as London, Birmingham or Manchester might record a list of species almost as high in number. On the whole,

Not many butterflies breed in gardens but many pass through and pause to sip nectar from flowers.

The common blue (left) and small copper (centre) are found all over the country, but the small skipper lives south of the Mersey and Humber. Skippers are unusual because they fold their wings flat like moths.

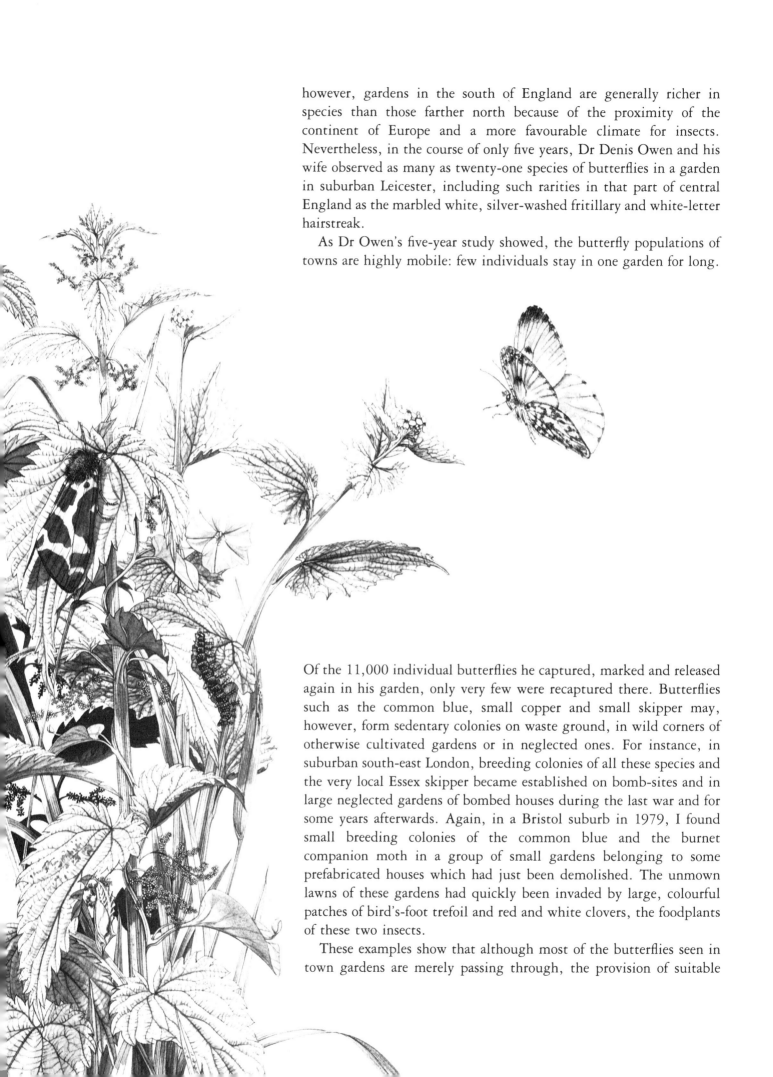

however, gardens in the south of England are generally richer in species than those farther north because of the proximity of the continent of Europe and a more favourable climate for insects. Nevertheless, in the course of only five years, Dr Denis Owen and his wife observed as many as twenty-one species of butterflies in a garden in suburban Leicester, including such rarities in that part of central England as the marbled white, silver-washed fritillary and white-letter hairstreak.

As Dr Owen's five-year study showed, the butterfly populations of towns are highly mobile: few individuals stay in one garden for long.

Of the 11,000 individual butterflies he captured, marked and released again in his garden, only very few were recaptured there. Butterflies such as the common blue, small copper and small skipper may, however, form sedentary colonies on waste ground, in wild corners of otherwise cultivated gardens or in neglected ones. For instance, in suburban south-east London, breeding colonies of all these species and the very local Essex skipper became established on bomb-sites and in large neglected gardens of bombed houses during the last war and for some years afterwards. Again, in a Bristol suburb in 1979, I found small breeding colonies of the common blue and the burnet companion moth in a group of small gardens belonging to some prefabricated houses which had just been demolished. The unmown lawns of these gardens had quickly been invaded by large, colourful patches of bird's-foot trefoil and red and white clovers, the foodplants of these two insects.

These examples show that although most of the butterflies seen in town gardens are merely passing through, the provision of suitable habitats even on a small scale may soon persuade at least some species other than the unwelcome large and small cabbage whites to stay and breed. An area of uncut grass, especially if it contains such wild species as annual meadow grass, cat's-tail, cock's-foot, Yorkshire fog and slender false brome, may easily entice such butterflies as the speckled wood, wall brown, hedge brown (gatekeeper), meadow brown, small heath, small skipper and large skipper, whose caterpillars are grass-feeders.

Most gardeners hate stinging nettles and eradicate them on sight, yet they are rich in nitrogen, phosphates, copper and other mineral salts, and properly managed actually enrich the soil and dispense with the need for artificial fertilizers. The old belief that where nettles grow the soil will yield fine crops is, in fact, correct. So there ought not to be any serious objection to maintaining a patch of nettles for those particularly beautiful butterflies, so fond of gardens, the small tortoiseshell, peacock, comma and red admiral, whose larval foodplant it is. Moreover, the stinging nettle is the foodplant of many other interesting insects, including such harmless and attractive moths as the beautiful golden Y, the burnished brass, the spectacle, the snout, garden tiger, mother-of-pearl and small magpie.

Orange-tip butterflies are seen in towns more often nowadays and, incidentally, are recolonizing parts of northern England and southern Scotland from which they disappeared many years ago. One of their favourite larval foodplants in the wild is jack-by-the-hedge or garlic mustard, which will often appear as a garden weed in suburban districts and is really pretty enough to be allowed to grow undisturbed along a garden hedge. However, several other plants belonging to the *Cruciferae* are cultivated in gardens, such as garden rock-cress, honesty and sweet rocket, and are alternative foodplants for the orange-tip. Its eggs are deposited beneath the flower heads of all these plants, the caterpillars later feeding upon the developing seed pods which they resemble to a remarkable degree.

THE LARGE AND small cabbage whites are, of course, unwanted and serious pests of cabbages; but there is another white butterfly, the green-veined white, which rarely attacks cabbages and although its caterpillars will feed on related cultivated flowers such as honesty, it does little, if any, damage in the garden. If they are available, the female prefers to lay her eggs on wild *Cruciferae* such as garlic mustard, charlock, lady's smock and various wild cresses. Being the same size as the small cabbage white, the green-veined is easily mistaken for it. When it is seen at rest, however, the mixture of black and yellow concentrated along the veins of the underside of the hind wings produces the characteristic 'green-veined' appearance. The green-veined white is, in fact, a pretty butterfly and worth encouraging.

The only other butterflies likely to breed in average-sized gardens, those other than country gardens, bordered with woodland and with

Some plants are very attractive to butterflies and moths. Stinging nettles (on the opposite page) are the food of peacock caterpillars and are also fed upon by the small tortoiseshell whose pupa is shown below. The garden tiger moth's boldly patterned wings make it easy to find. Its caterpillar is the well-known 'woolly bear'. The orange-tip (which is about to land) lays its eggs on honesty and other garden plants.

Overleaf: The peacock (top left) is feeding on the flower of a buddleia (sometimes called the butterfly bush) and the brimstone, named after its sulphur-yellow colour, is on a hydrangea. In the centre, there is a green-veined white, which prefers weeds to cabbages, and the abundant small tortoiseshell. The red admiral feeding on a blackberry flower is the most brilliantly patterned of the common butterflies. The wall butterfly (bottom right) likes to bask on sunny walls and on tree trunks.

other natural features) are the holly blue and, perhaps, the green hairstreak and the brimstone. Holly blues are usually as much at home in town parks and gardens as they are in the country, although their numbers do tend to fluctuate from year to year: occasionally they become quite rare after years of abundance, and then become common again. Except in Northern Ireland, there are two generations each year: the spring brood of caterpillars feeds on holly blossoms and the autumn brood consumes those of ivy. As ivy and holly are common in town and country gardens alike, it is not surprising that the holly blue is well adapted to both types. The green hairstreak is very unlikely to be found breeding in an urban garden, except, perhaps, on the extreme outskirts of a town, even if its foodplants of dogwood, broom, gorse, dyer's greenweed, bilberry (in the north) or bramble are present. On the other hand, it may well be found breeding in many country gardens or can be encouraged to do so. A garden—even a suburban one—containing a specimen or two of the brimstone butterfly's two food plants, alder buckthorn and purging buckthorn, might well entice a female to lay her eggs on their foliage. Brimstones are great wanderers; the males in particular often penetrate far into urban areas.

There are exceptions to every rule, of course, but these are the butterflies which one has a reasonable chance of persuading to breed in

the garden if the right foodplants and environmental conditions are provided. With moths there is much less difficulty. Many species lay their eggs upon a wide range of low-growing plants which are common 'weeds' in both town and country gardens. Thus, most gardens will have a considerable number of species breeding already. Unfortunately, there is not enough space in this chapter to mention more than a few that you can reasonably expect to find inhabiting your garden, even if you live in a large town or city. Readers living in the north of Britain or in Ireland must anticipate fewer species than those living in the climatically more favourable south of England. Nevertheless, they will be compensated to some extent by the occurrence of other species, such as the Scotch argus butterfly or the northern spinach moth, which are restricted to, or more common in, the north.

You may be able to coax more moths and butterflies of your choice to breed by providing those foodplants which are not already growing in your neighbourhood. Inevitably, the occurrence of a species in a particular garden naturally depends not only upon the region of the British Isles in which it is situated, but also upon the proximity of the garden to an area in which that species is breeding naturally. For example, a suburban garden situated not far away from a park or golf course with wild areas, or a piece of waste land, may expect regular visits from species which may be breeding there like the meadow brown, small heath and common blue butterflies, and the six-spotted burnet, burnet companion and Mother Shipton moths.

Incidentally, you may well be graced by a visit from a butterfly or moth not normally considered a garden species. For instance, I have seen a dark green fritillary in a suburban garden in Bristol, while Dr Owen once received a visit from a silver-washed fritillary in his garden in suburban Leicester; but neither butterfly could reasonably be included in a list of likely visitors to such gardens. Surprises are always bound to occur! I have seen a marsh fritillary in the middle of Oxford and a grayling in the heart of urban south-east London and, in 1968, some people were lucky enough to see monarchs in their suburban gardens during the remarkable immigration which took place that year of this famous North American long-distance butterfly.

SOME OF THE moths occurring naturally in an urban or suburban garden and, indeed, perhaps even a few of the butterflies, may constitute relict populations which have survived from the time before the houses were built and the gardens laid out. It is remarkable how tenacious some insects can be in holding on to the last vestiges of their original rural habitats. For example, in spite of a steady growth in the volume of bricks and mortar in heavily built-up parts of Bristol, the highly colourful cinnabar moth still manages to breed wherever its alternative foodplants, Oxford ragwort and stinking groundsel, grow in gardens, on waste bits of land or even in almost bare backyards and car parks.

Such tenacity has been helped, in some instances, by the survival as

The life-cycles of butterflies and moths can be watched by keeping them in a simple cage. All that is needed is a sheet of fairly stiff transparent plastic and a large tin. A toffee tin or a small biscuit tin is suitable. It is best if the lid fits over the rim of the tin. Roll the plastic sheet into a cylinder which fits snugly into the rim and secure it with sticky tape. Fit the lid over the top.

The butterflies or moths can be collected as eggs or caterpillars. Make a note of the plant on which they were found because it will be needed as food. The plant can be rooted in a small flower pot or cut stems can be kept in a vase of water. The latter may be best because caterpillars are greedy feeders and fresh leaves have to be supplied. Eventually the caterpillars pupate and, in due course, the adult insects emerge. Some caterpillars need soil to pupate in.

68

garden lawns of original pasture fields. Again in suburban Bristol, there is such a lawn with an adjacent sports field in the grounds of a school which has obviously been little altered since its enclosure as long ago as 1780. Such characteristic wild flowers of pasture as cowslips, bulbous buttercups, bird's-foot trefoil, hoary plantain, lesser celandine and self-heal still appear year after year, in spite of repeated mowings. Associated with the relict flora of this lawn and sports field are isolated colonies of meadow brown and small heath butterflies, latticed heath moth and two species of grass veneer moths of the family *Crambidae*, plus the meadow grasshopper, *Chorthippus parallelus*.

THE SMOKY WAINSCOT, silver ground carpet, common carpet, rivulet, lime-speck pug and common swift are other examples of moths which probably survive in many gardens as relicts from populations which once inhabited the original countryside of fields, hedgerows and small woods. On the three occasions that I have occupied a newly built house on farmland which had previously not been built on, I have been able to observe how various moths and other insects have succeeded in clinging on as long as remnants of the original grassland, hedgerows or the trees with which they were associated remained.

Some species vanish when the original habitat is dug up and the new gardens are laid out, and return when the gardens become established and mature, and their foodplants re-appear as weeds. Others, of course, invade the gardens from elsewhere attracted by the weeds or by certain native trees and their exotic allies planted intentionally by the gardener. The planting of crops such as cabbages, turnips, potatoes and so on, leads to the colonization of the new garden by pests; these may, in any case, be feeding in the neighbourhood on wild relatives of these plants. Then there are always those species which may pass through a garden on their way to somewhere else, often flying randomly; they may pause to feed at suitable flowers, but seldom stay long. Night-flying moths may be attracted from considerable distances by the bright lights of houses and street lamps. In fact, many of the moths which entomologists record in their gardens have been captured either because they flew into brightly lit rooms through open windows, or because they were deliberately attracted to moth traps, such as those illuminated, powerful mercury vapour lamp bulbs. These are especially attractive to moths and other nocturnal insects which are highly sensitive to the strong, long-wave beams of ultra-violet light which they emit.

Moths are drawn to electric light or candles basically because, when they happen to fly nearby, the special structures in their compound eyes react and cause them to become so disorientated that they are absolutely unable to maintain a straight line of flight. They are therefore deflected in ever-decreasing spirals towards and around the flames.

Butterflies and moths which migrate to the British Isles fall into the category of those species which may wander into gardens, but many of them may also stop to breed if they find the right foodplants and a suitable environment. In fact, one may expect to encounter a migratory insect almost anywhere—sometimes in quite unexpected places. Thus, an entomologist will be delighted, but not really surprised, to meet with a painted lady flying along London's Oxford Street or through Soho; or even to find a Camberwell beauty in Camberwell! Actually, the Camberwell beauty butterfly was so-named because the first British examples were seen flying in Camberwell in 1748 when it was still a village, and not, as it is now, a densely built-up suburb of south-east London.

Most of these migratory butterflies and moths consume vast amounts of energy on their long flights; so they need to refuel pretty often. Therefore, gardens with an abundance of flowers rich in nectar are highly attractive to them, irrespective of whether they are situated in the open countryside or in the heart of a city.

Now that we have discussed the plants which may attract *Lepidoptera* to breed in your garden, we can turn to those flowers which are most likely to invite them to feed in the adult or imago stage; and this will naturally lead on to discussion of the part these insects play in the pollination of garden plants and 'weeds'.

An average well-stocked garden often exceeds the surrounding countryside in the sheer diversity of its nectar- and pollen-bearing plants, particularly these days when the large-scale use of herbicides has deprived most farm fields of the profusion of wild flowers which used to delight the eyes of country ramblers in earlier and less efficient times. Therefore, gardens, whether in town or country, are now an important, if artificial habitat: apart from providing a sufficiently varied habitat to support a large population of breeding insects, they are a vital source of nourishment for those adult varieties which depend upon nectar. Incidentally, some butterflies and moths also feed upon the juices of rotting fruit as well as on the sweet honeydew secreted by the hordes of aphids which often infest gardens, in spite of the measures taken against them.

There are some moths, such as the swifts, which lack functional mouthparts and therefore do not feed at all in the adult state. There are also very small primitive moths of the family *Micropterigidae*, sometimes seen in gardens, which possess biting mouthparts for chewing pollen and are consequently unable to suck nectar. However, the majority of moths and all butterflies found in Britain imbibe nectar through mouthparts which have become specially modified to form a sucking tube. When not in use this proboscis or 'tongue' is coiled up under the head like a watch spring. It varies considerably in length in different species: in some—for example, the convolvulus hawkmoth—the tongues are very long, thus allowing deep tubular flowers to be probed.

A S WITH BEES and many other insects, nectar-seeking butterflies and moths have evolved a role in the pollination of a great many plants. Originally, pollination by insects was probably accidental: it occurred when insects such as beetles and primitive moths with biting mouthparts visited flowers to eat the highly nutritious pollen brought by the wind, or which was produced by self-pollinating plants. Some of the uneaten pollen adhering to the insect's body would have been transferred to other flowers of the same species when they, in turn, were visited. This process would have been aided by the tendency of such insects to continue visiting flowers of the same species rather than a random assortment. Since cross-fertilization by insects is more reliable than the more chancy method of wind dispersal of pollen, it paid plants to evolve flowers which were especially attractive to insects. Thus, they developed colourful blossoms within the colour range most readily seen by them (that is, especially the blue part of the spectrum), and alluring and distinctive scents to guide them to an alternative source of nourishment which was less wasteful of pollen as far as the plant was concerned—nectar.

Nectar consists of an energy-rich solution of various sugars; it is produced in special nectaries at the base of the flower. To keep the insects moving from flower to flower and transferring pollen as they go, only small quantities of nectar are released at a time in the nectaries. Moreover, to guide insects to the nectaries, flowers have evolved special markings or patterns which, as it were, point the way; although some of these are almost invisible to us, they are well within the parts of the light spectrum seen by an insect. Many plants pollinated by night-flying moths produce a stronger scent at night than during the day; some, like tobacco plants, have even evolved flowers and scents which cater specially for such nocturnal visitors.

It is clear, therefore, that if we wish to entice as wide a variety of adult butterflies and moths as possible to visit our gardens for food, then we must stock them with those plants which cater most

The large hawkmoths are a prize sight when they come out on warm summer evenings. They hover in front of tubular flowers and insert their long tongues to sip the nectar. This convolvulus hawkmoth is feeding at a convolvulus or bindweed. Hawkmoths are also attracted to cultivated plants with long corollas, such as honeysuckles and petunias.

71

successfully for their needs. Among the outstandingly attractive plants to *Lepidoptera*, are the heavily-scented buddleia (butterfly-bush) and the large pink-flowered ice-plant.

Anyone who wishes to encourage visits from some of the large and spectacular long-tongued hawk-moths must make sure that sweet-smelling, nectar-bearing flowers with long tubular corollas, such as honeysuckle, petunias and tobacco plants, are present. Even urban gardeners in the south of England can expect visits from the elephant, eyed, lime, poplar and privet hawks, while those elsewhere in the British Isles can at least anticipate seeing the most widespread British hawk-moth of all—the poplar hawk. In favourable years they might also see those migrants from southern Europe—the convolvulus and humming-bird hawks—as both these species sometimes penetrate to the farthest corners of the British Isles. Unfortunately, though, in most years they are rare.

The convolvulus hawk is one of the largest and most powerful of its family found in Britain, having a wing-span of between 12 and 13 centimetres (4½ and 5 inches), and an incredibly long proboscis (or tongue), some 12–13 centimetres (4½–5 inches) in length, which enables it to probe tubular flowers while hovering before them after dark. The much smaller, day-flying humming-bird hawk also has a long tongue; when extended into a flower this looks remarkably like the long, thin beak of a humming-bird. Indeed, the whole appearance of this handsome moth, as it hovers before a flower in the sunshine, with its rapidly beating wings merely an orange blur, large bird-like eyes and the long black, grey and white scales at the tip of the abdomen expanded to look like the tail of a bird, leads many people, unfamiliar with bird or moth, to think that they have actually seen a humming-bird wild in Britain. The humming-bird hawk is especially fond of feeding at the blossoms of buddleia, red valerian and old-fashioned dahlias; it should be approached cautiously, as a sudden movement on the part of the observer will send it darting away in a flash. However, if one waits a while, there is a good chance that it will return to the same flower.

The extremely beautiful elephant hawk-moth and the smaller, but equally lovely small elephant hawk may also be seen in gardens over most of the British Isles, with the exception of the northern half of Scotland. Unlike the elephant hawk, the smaller species is unlikely to be encountered in an urban garden. In some British towns and cities, such as London, the elephant hawk is now a genuinely urban insect, having colonized these places when one of its chief foodplants, rosebay willowherb, became established in abundance on bomb sites and in derelict gardens in World War II. Its very large caterpillars became exceptionally abundant for a time during the war and in the immediate post-war years until its chief enemies, certain parasitic ichneumon wasps and tachinid flies, found them and moved in as well. Now the elephant hawk-moths and their parasites have established a more balanced population, but remain quite common.

Owing to the popularity of its foodplants, privet and lilac, in town hedgerows and gardens respectively, the very large privet hawk is a common species in many urban areas in the south. When I was a boy in London, my friends and I used to find its huge caterpillars with ease by searching along the copings and pavements beneath the inevitable, uniformly trimmed Japanese or broad-leaved privet hedges for their big and easily recognized droppings. We would follow a trail of them until it ended with very fresh ones and there, in the hedge above, we

would find our fat, glossy apple-green quarry, with curved tail hook and violet-bordered white stripes on its body, arched in a stiff, defensive posture at our unwelcome intrusion.

The whitish-green caterpillars of the eyed hawk-moth belong to one of the few hawk-moth species likely to be found feeding in gardens all over the British Isles, except the north of Scotland, since they feed readily on apple trees, in addition to their more natural foodplants, poplars, sallows and willows. The moth gets its name from the strikingly blue eye-spots on each hind wing which are suddenly revealed under the covering forewings when the moth is disturbed at rest: in conjunction with the protruding, fat, snout-like body they cause the moth to take on the appearance of a small mammal with

A search of privet hedges in July and August may be rewarded by finding the 7.5 centimetre (3 inch) caterpillars of the privet hawkmoth. They may also be found on lilacs and other shrubs. The caterpillars descend to the ground and bury themselves in the soil when it is time to pupate. The adult moths emerge in the following June or July.

large staring eyes, with the result that would-be predators are startled and frightened away.

There are two garden moths that are particularly worth mentioning as they have only colonized Britain in the course of this century and are both associated with garden flowers: the golden plusia and the varied coronet. Both are rather small moths which have extended their breeding ranges northwards in Europe, presumably in response to the increased warmth of the climate which became most noticeable in the first half of this century. Their spread into Britain and northern Europe was made possible by the popularity of their larval foodplants in gardens there: delphiniums in the case of the golden plusia and sweet william and other cultivated dianthus in that of the varied coronet. The golden plusia was first seen in Britain in 1890; since then it has spread all over England, Wales and southern Scotland. It had even reached County Dublin by 1939. The varied coronet did not start to colonize Britain until 1948, but it has already spread over most of the southern and eastern counties of England. Several other moths have also recently colonized Britain, or are attempting to do so, from the European mainland. In their case, too, the reason is probably the increasing warmth of the climate. However, with the possible exception of Blair's shoulder-knot, whose larvae feed on the Monterey cypress, none is especially associated with gardens.

So far, no description has been given in this chapter of the evolution of a butterfly or moth. Basically, there are four stages in the life of these insects: egg; caterpillar (larva); chrysalis (pupa); and adult (imago). Thus, they are typical examples of those insects which undergo a complete metamorphosis. In contrast, insects such as grass hoppers and dragonflies have an incomplete one: on hatching from the egg, they gradually grow with each successive moult more and more like the adult without undergoing a pupal stage. The caterpillar or larva of a butterfly or moth, on the other hand, is obviously very dissimilar from the perfect insect in appearance and structure, and therefore needs to be completely reconstructed and transformed during its time as a pupa. The awesome process by which much of the caterpillar's body is broken down within the pupa into a sort of soup and then reassembled to form the body of the adult butterfly or moth—in many species within the space of three weeks or less—is one of the most astonishing happenings in Nature.

The golden plusia moth on larkspur, and the varied coronet on sweet William, are newcomers to Britain. The golden plusia arrived in England in 1890, having spread northwards through Europe, and the varied coronet appeared some years earlier.

Each time a caterpillar needs to moult, it stops feeding and attaches itself with silken threads to a leaf or twig. After a day or more, the old skin splits behind its head and along its back, and the caterpillar emerges to resume feeding, its new skin or cuticle soon hardening on contact with the air. When fully-fed and ready to pupate, it again ceases to feed, darkens in colour, and wanders about until it finds a suitable place for pupation. In many butterflies it spins a silken pad on the chosen leaf or twig, or other pupation site, and then hangs suspended from it by its last pair of legs (claspers). After several hours or even days, its skin begins to split behind its head and is shed by a series of wriggling movements. With many butterflies, the old skin is completely shed by a remarkable acrobatic manoeuvre in which, with a final violent wriggle, the suspended fresh pupa releases its hold of the silken pad, casts off the skin, and grasps the pad again, all in a flash. Some butterflies and most moths, however, retain their hold on the last shrivelled vestiges of the old skin. At first the pupa is very soft and vulnerable, but soon hardens and tends to assume colours and markings which harmonize with its surroundings.

The caterpillars of a few butterflies, such as the grayling, Scotch argus and some of the skippers, and many moths, spin a cocoon before they moult for the final time; depending upon the species, this may be composed purely of silken threads and perhaps hidden in a shelter of leaves or among dead leaves and other debris on the ground, or mixed with bits of leaf, bark or other available material which camouflage it perfectly among its surroundings. The immense variety of construction to be found in moth cocoons is a fascinating study in itself. Other moth caterpillars simply burrow into the soil and construct an earthen cell where they can pupate in safety.

Some species of butterflies and moths pass the whole of the winter as pupae, while others hibernate in the egg, caterpillar or adult stages. In

the latter cases, the pupal stage, occurring as it does in the warmer months, is often of quite short duration: usually from two to four weeks, depending upon the species. In the numerous species which produce more than one generation in a year, the duration of all these stages of development may, of course, vary.

When the perfect insects are within a few days of emerging, the pupal shells become soft and feel loose to the touch; and, mainly in the case of butterflies, the wing colour patterns begin to show through. The actual emergence is usually very fast, and the imago is often ready to fly within an hour or two. When it first appears, the wings are small, limp and crumpled, but as it hangs from some vantage point blood is pumped into them and they expand and stiffen rapidly. Before the adult insect flies off, it excretes a good deal of fluid containing the waste products left over from the chemical changes which took place in the pupa, and this dries quickly to a powder.

Many people believe that adult butterflies live only for a day: in fact, all British butterflies and most, if not all of the moths, have a potential life-span far longer than that. Again it depends upon the species and the season at which a particular generation of adults is on the wing: thus, in the small tortoiseshell, for example, the adult butterflies which appear in the spring have hibernated in buildings, hollow trees, etc., since the previous autumn and may well have lived for as long as ten months. They pair and lay eggs, giving rise to a second brood of butterflies in early summer which have a life expectancy of only two to three weeks; this life-span applies to most spring and summer broods of butterflies and probably to most adult moths which do not hibernate. Naturally, many individuals may not survive as long as that because of premature death due to predators or other causes. Another factor to be taken into account in assessing the life-spans of *Lepidoptera* is the prevailing weather: in warm conditions, conducive to constant activity, they may become worn out and die sooner than in unsettled weather when several wet and sunless days will be spent resting inactive in the vegetation. On the other hand, particularly cold, wet and generally unfavourable weather may cause heavier mortality than usual.

On the subject of mortality, occasional reference has been made in this chapter to the invariably fatal attacks of parasitic flies and wasps on the caterpillars of *Lepidoptera*. Although mention is made of them in the chapters dealing with bees, wasps and ants, and spiders and flies, it would be an omission to conclude this chapter without some account of the various ways in which they set about their seemingly cruel and ruthless but—in the interests of ecological stability—necessary work.

The parasitic flies belong to the family of *Diptera* known as the *Tachinidae* and are similar in appearance to house flies, blow-flies and their like. Most of the nearly 250 known British species attack the caterpillars of *Lepidoptera*, usually laying their eggs directly on the host's skin; on hatching, the fly grubs burrow into the caterpillar and feed within on its tissues. They manage to avoid killing their host until they are fully fed, upon which they bore their way out from what is left of its body and pupate near by. Some species of tachinid flies attach their eggs to the hairs of hairy caterpillars, from where the resulting larvae climb down to burrow into the body; others pierce the skin and lay eggs underneath; yet others, like *Gonia divisa*, deposit immense numbers of small eggs on turnips and other foodplants of the turnip moth so that its caterpillars ingest them while feeding, and are parasitized that way.

Many of the enormous number of species of parasitic wasps in the British Isles have similar life-histories to the tachinids, but they belong to three distinct groups; the *Braconidae*, the *Ichneumonidae* and the *Chalcidoidae*. The braconids include species which lay many eggs on a host and others which deposit only one, like the majority of the ichneumonids (ichneumons). The females of most species of ichneumons can be recognized by their often long, needle-like ovipositors through which they insert their eggs into the host. Chalcids, too, may have quite conspicuous ovipositors, but they are mostly tiny, often minute metallic coloured wasps; some even complete their life histories inside the eggs of insects. Other chalcid species attack the soft, freshly formed pupae of butterflies and moths, and yet others their caterpillars. So fantastic are the life-histories of these extraordinary little wasps, that in some species only a single egg is inserted in an egg, caterpillar or pupa of a host, yet it goes on dividing so that eventually not one, but up to a hundred or more chalcids may emerge from the host's sorry remains.

The small tortoiseshell spends the winter in protected corners and crevices, so that it is one of the first butterflies to be seen in the spring. The eggs are laid on the underside of stinging nettle leaves and the plants later become infested with swarms of caterpillars. A new generation of adult butterflies emerges in late summer and they become the most abundant butterfly in the garden.

Bees,Wasps and Ants

The insects whose lives are discussed in this chapter belong to a huge group called *Hymenoptera*. All members of this group hatch from an egg as a grub which, when fully grown, often spins itself a cocoon in which it undergoes a transformation from grub to pupa (the equivalent of the chrysalis of a moth or butterfly) and then from pupa to adult. Adult insects—with certain exceptions like the worker caste of ants which are wingless—have two pairs of wings of which the back pair is smaller than the front and is coupled to them in flight by a row of tiny hooks. Hymenopteran grubs are generally unenterprising and the story of *Hymenoptera* is best understood from the aspect of the female insect trying to do her best for her relatively helpless offspring or, as we shall see later, of sterile females caring for their younger sisters while being themselves incapable of laying eggs. Male *Hymenoptera* are almost without exception totally unconcerned with the well-being of their descendants.

Among the most active insects in the garden are a group of species known as the solitary wasps. They frequent areas of bare ground, such as steep, sandy banks or trodden paths. In such places a mother wasp can excavate with her jaws and legs the deep burrows destined to be the nurseries of her grubs, for the solitary species make careful provision for their young. One of these dutiful mothers is the spider wasp. She is smaller and more slender than the yellow-and-black social species and, apart from a red waistband, entirely black. Even her

Apart from the familiar stinging, food-pilfering wasps, there are a number of harmless species which have a solitary life-style. The black wasps drill holes in posts or other wood and stock them with the bodies of flies and other small insects which are later eaten by the wasps' larvae. The digger wasps on the flowers make their nests in burrows in sandy soil. The ruby-tail wasp, shown looking into one of the holes, is a parasite which lays its eggs in the provisions laid up by other species.

wings are a smoky colour and she often buzzes them as she runs about the ground in the sunshine, dashing hither and thither and occasionally making short flits from pebble to pebble. Suddenly she sees a spider. In the same moment the spider, sensing danger, freezes on the spot. Unfortunately, this trick of stopping dead and remaining motionless, which often saves it from attack by birds and lizards, is of no avail here. A quick pounce, a lightning jab with her sting and the wasp has the spider paralyzed. The victorious wasp then drags her helpless prey along the ground towards her chosen nest site. When she is close to it, she lodges the spider in a convenient place, such as the leaf-axil of a grass stem, where it is relatively safe from the attention of ants, and rushes off to inspect the nest site. If she has already started a nest hole, this will be re-opened, having been closed by her before departure on her hunting trip in such a way as to be invisible to possible enemies. Some spider wasps wait until they have caught the first spider before digging the nest shaft, while others, with greater optimism, prepare one before starting the hunt. In either case, since

several spiders are to be entombed in each hole, the entrance must be stopped and re-opened a number of times. If she is satisfied that all is well on her return, the wasp returns to the parked spider and drags it inside. When she has stored sufficient spiders in the hole to feed one of her grubs for the whole of its life, she lays a single egg on one of the victims and stops up the entrance for the last time. The grub soon hatches from the egg and consumes the spiders one after another; since they are paralyzed, not dead, they stay fresh and unputrefied until required. Like all wasp and bee grubs, this one grows very rapidly and is soon ready to turn into a pupa. It does not appear above ground as an adult wasp until the following spring.

SPIDER-HUNTING WASPS are just a few of scores of hunting wasps. Many are confined to sandy heathland and dunes and are rarely encountered in the garden. Others, such as the little black wasps, are found almost everywhere. Some black wasps make their tiny nest holes in wooden posts or dead branches, often taking advantage of a nail hole or a woodworm beetle's exit hole to get started, while others bore into the soft pith of blackberry canes. They provision their burrows with small flies or moths, or even leafhoppers and greenfly, the type of prey depending on the species of wasp. Close scrutiny of the 'worm holes' in a wooden post in a sunny position in summer will often reveal that some are occupied by black wasps, whose little faces can be seen in the entrances. The need of a black wasp to guard the entrance of its hole is a pressing one as any store of food is a temptation to all manner of thieves and parasites. Among the latter are the beautiful ruby-tail wasps. Ruby-tails are a metallic blue-green or yellow-green and their abdomens usually have a reddish sheen, glinting like shot silk as the sunlight catches them. They enter unguarded burrows of a variety of solitary wasps to lay their eggs on the stored provisions, and the solitary wasps' labour then serves only to raise a brood of insect cuckoos.

Whenever one hears the word 'wasp' without a qualifying epithet, the mind's eye sees the familiar black and yellow ruffians who invade the baker's shop window and disrupt picnic parties. These are the worker caste of the social species of wasps. We have five species of them in Britain, all looking very much alike and leading similar lives. Their colonies are annual, being established in spring and dying out in autumn. Only the fertile females survive the winter. They may be encountered hibernating alone, perhaps in a folded sack in the garden shed or hanging immobile in a fold of the curtains of a little-used spare room, holding on to the fabric with tightly closed jaws. The warmth and lengthening days of spring tempt the over-wintered female wasps into activity. Each refreshes herself with a sip or two of nectar from a convenient flower and sets about finding a suitable place to build a home which, with luck, will grow into a populous city with her as its queen.

The female selects a site which may be a mouse hole in the ground

As well as the familiar wasps, honeybees and bumblebees, a variety of small wasps and bees come into the garden. They are called 'solitary' wasps and bees because they do not live in large colonies with queens and workers. Each female of a solitary species lays her eggs in a small nest and she leaves provisions for the grubs to feed on. The nests are made by excavating burrows in soil or soft rock and in natural holes, and these insects will use artificial 'nest boxes'. Acceptable artificial nest sites include bundles of drinking straws or lengths of bamboo, plugged at one end, holes drilled in posts and old logs and airbricks.

A common visitor will be the red osmia bee, which looks like a small, reddish honeybee; she provisions her nest with honey and pollen. The leafcutter bees bring sections cut out of leaves and the solitary wasps provision their nests with caterpillars, spiders and other animals which they paralyse with their stings.

Honeybees have a very well organised society. When a worker finds a good source of food, she communicates its whereabouts to other bees in the nest. This can be demonstrated by luring a bee from a flower on to a twig dipped in honey and transferring her to a plate with a pool of honey or sugar-water. Mark her with a small blob of nail varnish and watch for her to return with more bees.

or the underside of a branch of a tree. The exact position varies: some species prefer a subterranean home while others habitually nest in trees, but a dense bush or a dark recess may serve equally well. Having chosen the site, the female wasp goes in search of building materials. She finds a sound, dry, wooden board or post—the garden fence will do nicely—and proceeds to scrape wood fibres from its surface with her jaws, moistening the wood with her saliva to facilitate the process. Soon she has between her jaws a pellet of wood pulp which she carries back to her chosen site where she plasters it on the underside of a firm support—a tree-root crossing the roof of an abandoned mouse nest, say. Back she goes for more wood pulp until she has constructed a delicate paper shell like half an eggshell with the open end facing downwards. This is filled with half a dozen paper cells, also facing downwards, in each of which she glues an egg. The work of building and enlarging the nest goes on but the female soon has the additional duty of hunting for small insects with which to feed the grubs which hatch from this first batch of eggs. The grubs grow rapidly and their mother brings in larger prey as soon as they can deal with it.

At this stage, many an overworked mother wasp succumbs to predators and the grubs perish, leaving the little inverted paper cup as a monument to what might have been. If all goes well, however, the full-grown grubs spin themselves cocoons in which they undergo the transition to adult wasps. When they emerge they look like smaller versions of their mother. All are female but their femininity is structural, not functional. They are sterile and will never lay eggs to reproduce their kind, although each is equipped with a sting. Oddly enough this fearsome weapon is a badge of femininity: it is a modification of the egg-laying tools of the plant-eating and parasitic relatives of wasps and bees. It is so highly modified in hunting wasps, social wasps and bees that even mother wasps and bees cannot use their sting for its original purpose of laying eggs. The egg-channel bypasses the sting completely.

WHEN THE FIRST half dozen wasps of the new generation emerge from their cocoons, they find that their mother is already rearing a new batch of grubs. They begin to gather food for these grubs and also bring in new wood pulp to extend the family home. The female, mother of all the wasps that will be born in the paper city during the course of the year, can now truly be called a queen. She is too precious to the colony to be exposed to the dangers of the outside world and as soon as there are sufficient worker wasps to run the home and do the foraging, she ceases going out and devotes herself entirely to the business of laying eggs. By the end of the season, the nest will be the size of a football, with six to ten floors of paper cells, all facing downwards towards the small entrance hole at the bottom and containing at the height of its development tens of thousands of individuals.

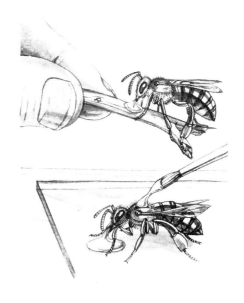

By late summer, foraging activity is fast and furious. If a cabbage patch is nearby, the caterpillars of the cabbage white butterflies will be slaughtered, cut up and carried home for the ravenous grubs. The gardener smiles benignly on the useful wasps and strolls over to his beehive, where his opinion quickly changes as he sees his beloved bees on the doorstep of their home meeting the same fate as the hapless caterpillars. The social wasps, unlike the solitary kinds, take just about anything that moves and even things that do not, provided that they are reasonably fresh. This readiness to take whatever comes is a key element in their ecological success.

With an abundance of food coming into the nest, certain changes affect the population. Males are reared and so are big, fertile females, as big as their mother and fully capable of laying as many eggs when their time comes. Neither the males nor the big females help their little sisters in the work of nest enlargement or brood rearing, taking all the advantages that the nest has to offer and, eventually, drifting off into the outside world to disport themselves on flowers.

Back at the ancestral home, demoralization sets in as summer ripens into autumn. The new generation of males and fertile females has been launched into the world and there is little point in working any more. The grubs are neglected, even murdered in their cells and eaten, and the once industrious workers idle away the golden days, getting drunk on the fermented juice of rotten fruit. Then one night there is a sharp frost and it is all over. Not quite over, though, because in various piles of sacks and undisturbed curtains sleeps the new generation of females of whom the lucky few will become, for a few brief weeks, queens of next summer's paper cities. When the world was young, or at least not much more than middle-aged, there appeared a race of social wasps who, like the spider-hunters, dug underground burrows and did most of their hunting on the surface of the soil. In the interests of economy the workers of this race abandoned wings entirely, leaving flight to the privileged few who were concerned with the business of reproduction. The ant was born. Life in narrow, winding, subterranean passages and among grass stems requires a lithe, flexible body, so many ants have two-jointed waists with a little hump of body between the two joints, like a spacer bead in a necklace. The exceptions go even further, having three waists and two consecutive spacer beads between the thorax and main part of the abdomen.

The three-waisted ants are represented in almost every garden by one or more rather long-bodied, strongly armoured, reddish coloured species, whose sharp stings frequently remind the unwary that they are related to bees and wasps. Two-waisted ants lack a sting, though their workers are all sterile females and might be expected to have the raw materials for one. They rely on their jaws and their ability to squirt a spray of acid at their enemies. For their nest sites the red stinging ants choose places that require little or no heavy digging, such as the space under a flat stone or the gap between the trunk of a dead tree and its loose bark. They mostly forage for animal food, although some also climb flowering plants to sip the nectar or to obtain from greenfly their sugary excreta, called honeydew.

Often their nests are exposed by gardening operations, when it can be seen that the colonies comprise rather few individuals and may have more than one queen. Eggs, grubs of various sizes and pupae are all neatly sorted into separate groups. The pupae are naked, red ants having apparently abandoned the ancestral habit of spinning cocoons. The helpless pupae, grubs and eggs are caught up by the agitated workers, and in a few minutes there is nothing to show that there was once a nest there, the whole colony having decamped to a safer site. Sometimes one may see a straggling line of red ants carrying their brood with them, engaged in moving house when they have outgrown the old one or when it has become unsuitable for some other reason. Occasionally, they may be seen carrying in their jaws the seeds of violets or pansies, which are carried to the nests for the sake of the little piece of oil tissue attached to each seed.

The most conspicuous garden ant is the black ant. Black ants are given to running about on paths in the sunshine and climb trees in order to obtain honeydew from the greenfly living there. Their colonies teem with countless thousands of individuals. The nest is usually headed by a single queen. Its passageways penetrate deep into the soil but large chambers may be excavated against the undersides of flagstones. Into these shallow chambers are piled hundreds or thousands of pupae, each enclosed in a cocoon. The cocoons which contain pupae of fertile females are several times larger than those of males and workers.

When the sun shines on their flagstone roofs, the shallow chambers are warmer than the deeper passages of the nest and the extra warmth hastens the development of the brood. Black ants are omnivorous, the

The wasps we commonly see are the workers from a large colony. They gather a variety of plant or animal and plant food which they take back to the nest to feed the queen and her large brood of larvae.

brood being fed mostly on insect food and the adults feeding largely on honeydew. Ants are extremely possessive about the territory around their nests and their favourite hunting grounds, and contest the ground fiercely against rival colonies, using the same weapons, jaws and acid spray, that they use against their prey. Apparently friend and foe are distinguished by the sense of taste, located in the antennae ('feelers'). Two ants meeting casually as they go about their business tap each other lightly with their antennae and, if they are from the same nest, pass on, perhaps exchanging a morsel of food as a token of friendship. When ants from different nests meet, the outcome of the encounter varies with the circumstances. If both parties are on exploratory forays they shy away from each other and avoid further contact. If one has wandered into the territory of another, it will usually beat a hasty retreat unless its own colony is bent on expansion, in which case a skirmish takes place, reinforcements from both sides hurry up and war is declared. A weak colony may be overrun and destroyed by a stronger neighbour but usually only small tracts of territory change hands in such engagements.

In early August, usually on the first hot day of the month, frenzied activity is seen around the entrances of the nests. This is the great day of the ants' year and normal work almost ceases. In early or mid-afternoon the males and reproductive females appear. Both sexes are winged. The males are not much bigger than the workers but the females are huge in comparison with their sterile sisters. All the nests over a wide area, often hundreds of square miles, erupt their winged forms into the air at the same time. Mating takes place in mid-air and the fertilized females drop to the ground. They will never need their wings again so they shed them and each female seeks a secluded place in which to found a new colony. Old colonies, unlike those of the social wasps, persist for a dozen or so years under the sway of the same queen, so there is no end-of-season tragedy for the ants. They tidy up the nest and settle down to see out the coming winter.

While all species of ants are social insects, the great majority of bees, like the majority of wasps, are individualists. The most numerous group is that which comprises the mining bees. Many of them make their burrows in banks or in trodden paths, but the most familiar species, the tawny mining bee, draws attention to herself by sinking her nest-shaft in lawns. The female is rather like a hive bee in shape and size but her furry coat is a bright, foxy red. The male is brown. The nest-shaft is sunk vertically into the ground and then branches into a mass of chambers. Each chamber is filled with a cake of pollen mixed with nectar, on to which a single egg is laid. Pollen is nutritious, rich in protein, and the grubs grow rapidly. The new generation of adult bees does not emerge until the following spring, when they open up the shaft to the surface; all winter it has remained closed against the weather. Although each female bee makes her own separate nest, many will nest close together in favoured spots and their progeny, emerging in the spring, leave hundreds of holes in the lawn, each surrounded by a conical spoil-heap of soil thrown out by the erstwhile inhabitants.

Many species of mining bees are plagued by homeless bees, wasp-

like creatures whose females can often be seen hanging about the groups of nest-holes and occasionally popping in and out of them. They lay their eggs on the pollen cakes intended for the grubs of the mining bees and their own young develop on the stores assiduously gathered by the architect of the nest.

Related to mining bees are leaf-cutter bees and their allies, which burrow in soft, rotten wood, nail-holes in posts, etc. They have been known to select such inconvenient sites as the cavity inside a door-lock, which the female bee entered via the keyhole, and the overflow pipe of a cistern. The common leaf-cutter looks like a broader, flatter version of the hive bee. When she is gathering food to store for her offspring she cannot be mistaken for a hive bee worker because she carries the precious load of pollen on a series of brushes on the underside of her abdomen. Hive bees and bumble bees carry the pollen in a pair of 'baskets' on the hind legs.

As in all bees, leaf-cutter grubs are fed on the standard mixture of

Bumblebee queens are the first insects to be seen in the early days of spring. They make their nests in old mouse holes or under piles of grass, but continue to collect pollen and nectar until sufficient workers have been reared to take over this task. Later, in the summer, male bumblebees patrol in large circles and mark leaves with scent to attract young queens, who will be the only survivors next spring.

pollen and nectar. It is stored in a series of cells laid end to end in the unbranched burrow in packages, each sufficient for the nourishment of a single grub. The first egg laid, the oldest, is the one at the end of the tunnel farthest from the entrance and the eggs nearer to the entrance are progressively younger. Yet in the spring it is the youngest bee that emerges first, reverse order to the sequence in which the eggs were laid. Presumably each bee waits until the cell next to it is empty before biting its way out of its own, but how it knows that the exit is clear is a mystery. The cells of the common leaf-cutter are lined with oval pieces of leaves and are separated from each other by discs of the same material. Unfortunately, in her anxiety to use only the best materials for the walls of her offsprings' cells, the mother bee has discovered that the leaves of hybrid tea roses are ideal. From these, or more rarely from the leaves of other roses or even strawberries, she cuts out her discs and ovals with a speed and precision impressive to watch. Each piece is carried home between her legs. It is a pleasure to watch this busy little insect at work, and because she flies slowly with her burden, she can be followed back to her nest and her activities there kept under observation.

A relative of the leaf-cutter bee collects the hairs from the surfaces of the leaves of downy plants, tearing them off with her jaws and rolling them into a ball between her legs. When she gets them home she uses them to line her burrow, embedding it in her cakes of pollen, each of which is enveloped in an impervious membrane. This provides a snug home for her growing family, but it can make a mess of ornamental plants, leaving untidy hairless patches on their leaves. Such is the love that certain admirers of the solitary bees have for the objects of their study that they often grow a few particularly downy plants in the hope of attracting this diligent creature to their gardens.

EVERYBODY KNOWS THE bumble bee and not a few admit to a certain fondness for it. People who have no compunction about swatting wasps and stamping on beetles may feel moved to rescue a drowning bumble bee from the water butt, particularly if nobody else is watching. In part, this affection is due to the bees' brightly coloured, furry, chunky bodies and in part to admiration for all the hard work they put in for the benefit of their community. In comparison with bumble bees, the hive bee is rather lazy. Bumble bees get up earlier in the morning and work in worse weather and later into the night. In a bad summer a colony of hive bees may do no more than 'tick over' in the expectation of better things to come. Bumble bee colonies, being annual, have to produce a new generation of queens before winter comes, no matter how bad the weather is.

There are about seven widespread species of bumble bees. Two are all black except for the 'tail end', which is red; four are black with yellow bands and of these, two have white tails, one has a buff tail and one has a pink tail. The seventh species is entirely brown with the fur on the thorax brighter and paler than that on the rest of the body. The

pink-tailed species is generally first to appear
in the spring. Males are usually coloured
differently from females. Workers and
queens are coloured alike.

The life-cycle is very similar in all species of
bumble bees. The over-wintered females establish
their nests in abandoned mouse nests or other
naturally occurring holes in the ground, or even on
the surface in piles of grass cuttings or in old birds'
nests. Having selected the site, the queen bee
constructs a large cell in which she makes a cake of the
traditional pollen-honey mixture and a smaller
container for honey alone. She lays a few eggs on the
cake, usually between six and twelve, and closes the roof
over them. Both this nursery and the honey pot are
constructed of wax secreted between the plates of her
abdomen, and softened and shaped by chewing with her
jaws. As the grubs grow, the mother bee fetches more food
for them, introducing it into the nursery by tearing a hole in
the roof each time and resealing it. When she is not out
gathering food, she sits on top of the brood cell. When they
are fully fed, the grubs spin themselves individual cocoons and
their mother is free to start rearing another brood on a
fresh pollen cake. The first worker bees to emerge from
their cocoons are very small, even compared with the
average size of worker bees, but they set to work with a will
to help rear further groups of brood. For a while, there are
both queen bees and workers flying in the spring, jostling
with one another on the flowers. Soon, only worker bees are to
be seen in the open, there being now enough of them in each nest

The tawny mining bee (left) is an excellent pollinator of fruit trees. Its sting is too weak to penetrate human skin, so it would be an entirely beneficial insect were it not for its habit of nesting in lawns. The females dig deep burrows by pulling earth out backwards and brushing it out with the hind feet; but it is not this which untidies the lawn since they make their tunnel entrances inconspicuous by scattering the earth.

All bees feed on nectar, and most have long 'tongues' with which to suck it from flowers. They feed their young on pollen mixed with honey. The tawny mining bee female digs a cell at the end of her tunnel and provisions it with a ball of honey and nectar. Each ball requires six or more journeys to flowers, and on each journey she transports half her own weight of pollen. When one cell is provisioned she lays an egg on the food ball, seals the cell and begins another cell higher up the tunnel. By the end of June the females have finished their work, closed up the burrow entrances and died. It is their progeny emerging the following spring that leave the lawn in a mess.

to do all the foraging necessary to feed the growing families of each queen. New brood cells, honey pots and special containers for pollen are constructed with wax secreted by the workers, and groups of empty cocoons are also pressed into service to store food not immediately required by the colony. Later in the year males and potential new queens are reared.

Mating takes place in summer and the mated females feed from summer and autumn flowers to build up a reserve of fat in their bodies to help them over-winter. They search out secluded spots in which to hibernate. The males and workers die off and the old nests fall silent. If one of these nests is opened in the autumn it is possible to tell how many bees have been reared in it by counting the empty cocoons. The total population of the nest is rarely more than a few hundred, in some cases much less. Cocoons are never reused for rearing another grub, nor are they ever destroyed.

It is not within the scope of this chapter to deal in detail with the life of the most advanced of the social bees, the honeybee, but a few words on foraging and swarming may not be out of place. A honeybee out foraging gathers nectar and pollen from only one kind of flower at a time. The nectar is carried home in her stomach and is regurgitated into a cell in the honeycomb where it is converted to honey by certain digestive juices with which it is mixed. The pollen is combed off her fur by various devices on her legs and is carried home in a pair of 'baskets' on her hind legs. At home, the pollen from different flowers is mixed together, which makes the specialized foraging seem rather pointless. A bee finding a new source of food naturally enough smells of the perfume of the flowers on which she has been working. If there is a lot of food available, she returns home in a very excited state which

alerts the other bees in the hive to the discovery. Her fellow bees now know that a good source of food is available and they also know its odour. She proceeds, by an intricate series of movements, to convey to them the direction and distance of the food supply. This ability is not shared by bumble bees and social wasps. The ants crawling on the ground mark their trails with little spots of a smelly substance, unique to each colony, which guide their fellows along the track in much the same way that explorers in a forest mark their way by cutting blazes on tree trunks. It works well, but compared with the honeybee's system it looks very primitive.

Honeybee colonies are perennial and, in fact, potentially immortal. The queen is quite incapable of founding a colony by herself, so the normal method of increasing the number of colonies is swarming. At times, usually in the months of May to July, new queens are raised in the hive. These fly away to meet males (called drones) from their own or another colony, and return fertilized to the hive. One of these mated females is chosen as a successor to the old queen. The deposed monarch, accompanied by a few thousand of her more loyal subjects, leaves the hive and this mass of bees, the swarm, settles on a convenient tree or bush in a dense cluster. From this temporary lodging scouts are sent out to prospect for a suitable site in which to found a new home. Hollow trees, chimneys and roof spaces of houses are among the favoured places. Swarms usually leave the hive in the morning and remain in a cluster for a day or more.

Beekeepers seem invariably to be pleasant and interesting people to meet. Perhaps because their lives have been enriched by getting to know and understand at least one small corner of the wonderful world of insects.

The honeybee (right) is the most social of the bees, living in permanent colonies hundreds of thousands strong. Each community consists of drones (males) whose sole purpose is to fertilize the queen, and who die after doing so; a queen, whose purpose is to lay eggs; and workers (sterile females whose ovipositors have been replaced by stings) who do all the work of the hive, cleaning and defending it, and feeding the queen, the drones and the larvae. Only the workers have the hairy pollen baskets on their hind legs which enable them to collect pollen and transport it back to the hive, so it is the worker honeybees that are so conspicuously busy around the garden as they labour to provision the combs and collect food for the rest of the community.

The workers have wax-secreting organs and they build the wax cells for honey-storage in which the larvae develop. Eggs to produce queens are laid in large round cells; those to produce workers are laid in the typical smaller hexagonal cells. Royal larvae are fed with royal jelly, a richer food than the worker larvae enjoy.

Beetles and Bugs

Unlike flies, moths, wasps and their relatives, most beetles and bugs go about their day-to-day business on foot, reserving flight for dispersal and migration. Because of this, they are easier to watch in the garden, and take more kindly to captivity in small observation cages. This makes many of them ideal objects of study for both naturalists and biologists.

There are two major distinctions between beetles and bugs. First, there is the way in which the insect develops from egg to adult. Bugs hatch from the egg as a smaller, wingless form of the adult. The growing bug moults a number of times (usually five), and with each moult becomes gradually more like the adult. If the individual is going to have wings when fully grown, small pads appear after the second moult in the position of the adult wings and become larger with each moult that follows. From the beetle egg, however, a grub emerges; usually it has three pairs of small legs and very short antennae. Like the young bug, this grub moults several times during its development but, instead of becoming more and more like the adult with each moult, it simply becomes a larger and larger grub. When it has eaten its last meal as a grub it moults again and becomes a non-feeding pupa, in which the form of the adult is clearly visible.

This pupa is similar to the chrysalis of a moth or butterfly except that the future wing cases, wings, legs and antennae are not fixed to its sides. After a resting stage, during which the internal parts are reorganized into the form needed by the adult beetle, the adult emerges from the skin of the pupa, its wings and wing cases expand, and the whole skin hardens as the adult colour develops. This process is particularly easy to watch in ladybirds because the mature grub does not hide in the soil to pupate like most beetle larvae, but turns into a pupa on the plant where it is living. The change can be witnessed in most gardens on a hot summer afternoon.

The second main difference between bugs and beetles is the way in which they feed. Bugs, at all stages of their lives, have mouth parts modified for sucking up liquid food. From the underside of the head arises a usually long and jointed tube called the rostrum. Down the middle of this tube, hidden in a deep groove, slide two pairs of very fine, flexible stylets. When the tip of the rostrum comes into contact with suitable food, either plant or animal, the stylets shoot out through a hole at the tip of the rostrum, pierce it and inject saliva through another canal running close to the salivary canal. Beetles have mouthparts adapted for biting and chewing, and are able to deal with solid food. All beetles, both as grubs and adults, have a pair of jaws which vary in size from the large and conspicuous mandibles of the carnivorous ground beetle to the tiny jaws at the tip of the slender, rigid snout of the plant-feeding weevils. If you cannot decide whether you are watching a beetle or a bug, your doubts will be resolved as soon as it begins to feed. The bugs most likely to be mistaken for beetles are shieldbugs. In addition to piercing mouthparts, shieldbugs have antennae which, although they are about the same length as the legs, consist of only five long segments; beetles usually have a dozen or so.

Shieldbugs are among the largest and most brightly coloured of the true bugs. The pied shieldbug, is very common on white deadnettle in spring and can be easily recognized by its striking black and white coloration. A slightly smaller relative is the woundwort shieldbug which lives on hedge woundwort. It is speckled grey and brown with most of the underside and a semicircular patch on the back, deep, coppery red. It was a rare insect in the nineteenth century but, for reasons which are not understood, has now become abundant in the southern half of England. On birch trees lives another shieldbug, called the parent bug because of the unusual behaviour of the adult female. When she has laid a group of eggs on a birch leaf, she remains with it instead of abandoning it as most insect mothers do. She protects the eggs from interference by placing herself between them and any danger and even remains with her newly hatched young ones for a few days.

A colourful member of the shieldbug family is the brassica bug which is black with a blue or green metallic tinge, pale rings on its legs and cream or red spots on the back. A close relative, the cuckoo flower bug, is pillarbox red with black markings. Both of them feed on plants of the cabbage and cress family. All of the shieldbugs mentioned so far are plant-feeders but there are a few carnivorous kinds with a special liking for caterpillars and grubs. Two such predators are the blue bug, long and bright metallic blue all over, and the caterpillar bug which is larger than the other species mentioned. It is brown with red legs and with two sharp spikes projecting sideways

Two of the commonest shieldbugs are the pied (left) which can often be seen on white deadnettles in spring, and the woundwort (right). Many of these bugs have stink glands which they use for defence, hence their alternative name, stink bugs. The pied shieldbug is one of the rare examples of an insect caring for its young. The female lays about fifty eggs in a shallow hole, which she digs in the ground. She watches over them, occasionally turning them with her beak, and when the tiny nymphs hatch, she leads them to the food plant. Once they begin to feed, she ceases to care for them.

Leaf-hoppers are extremely active leaping bugs related to the cicadas. They are mostly small, all vegetarians, and very varied in shape, form and coloration. One of the brightest coloured is the rhododendron leaf-hopper which can be seen in swarms on rhododendron bushes from April to October in the south of Britain. It is not a native insect, but was introduced from America about 1935. Both the young leaf-hoppers and the adults feed on the leaves of wild and cultivated rhododendrons, sucking their sap and thereby helping to spread a fungus disease called Bud Blast, which causes the flower buds to turn brown and die off without opening.

from the front part of the body. It is found particularly on oak bushes, while the blue bug lives on low plants or on the ground.

Two other kinds of predatory bugs, both of which are common on perennials and shrubs, are the common flower bug and the common damsel bug. The flower bug is very small and brightly coloured. Like many true bugs including the shieldbugs, the flower bug has only the last one-third of its forewings transparent and membranous; the rest is toughened like the wing-cases of beetles. When the wings are folded over the body, the membranous areas overlap. There is a bold, black spot in the middle of the toughened part of each forewing. The food of these bugs consists of creatures smaller than themselves, such as greenfly and mites. For some reason, flower bugs may sometimes stick their stylets into the skin of humans, particularly if the skin is warmed by the sun. Although the perforation made by the bug is tiny, enough saliva is injected into the skin to cause a pain which to some people is as severe as the pain of a bee sting. The grey-brown damsel bugs are larger than flower bugs, but more delicate in appearance, with long, slender appendages.

OFTEN THE OBSERVANT gardener will notice that the young leaves of some of his plants are distorted and tattered, perforated by numerous small, irregular holes. This is the work of capsid bugs, which feed on buds just as they are opening. As the leaves expand, the little holes expand as well, so that the appearance of the leaf is spoilt out of all proportion to the tiny amount of food consumed by the bugs. There are over two hundred different kinds of capsid bugs in Britain; most are soft-bodied and delicate, and many are brightly coloured. Some species are plant-feeders, others feed on animal food (usually other insects) and yet others have a mixed diet. If one leg is seized by an enemy, such as an ant, capsid bugs are able to break that leg off voluntarily and escape on the other five – an ability shared by harvest-spiders and similar to the well-known ability of lizards to shed their tails to escape from their enemies. Unlike the lizard's tail, however, the capsid's leg cannot grow again.

In the summer, the little lumps of froth called cuckoo-spit can be found on almost every kind of plant. If the froth is gently wiped away, or if a straw is poked into it, a soft-bodied green bug will be found living within the foam. The little creature, deprived of its froth, is in danger of drying out. If it is left unmolested it will quickly apply its rostrum to the plant stem or leaf on which it is standing, and begin to suck up the sap. Very soon a bubble will appear at the hinder end of the body. Then another bubble will form, and another, until the insect is again completely covered with froth to keep it cool and moist. When the cuckoo-spit bug is ready to undergo its final moult, it blows a large bubble around itself which eventually bursts, leaving the insect exposed to the air and surrounded by a ring of froth. It quickly moults and hardens off to become a froghopper.

The adult insect is about 6 millimetres ($\frac{1}{4}$ inch) long and can

jump strongly. There are about ten distinct colour patterns in the common froghopper, and a ten-minute search in high summer can reveal about half a dozen of them in the average herbaceous border. A less common but very striking relative is the wounded froghopper. It is about half as long again as its relative and is black with three big, blood-red spots on each of the toughened forewings. It is rather local in its distribution and varies in numbers from year to year. It needs areas where the ground is left undisturbed because the young stages live underground in groups, each one surrounded by a ball of stiff foam. These young stages feed on sap which they suck from plant roots.

Sometimes, when passing a rhododendron bush in summer or autumn, you may hear a rattling sound as dozens of insects, each resembling a rather slender froghopper, leap into the air, circle round and fly back to the bush. A more cautious approach to one of these insects will enable you to see that it is coloured bright green, yellow and red. This is the rhododendron leafhopper, a member of a large group of bugs which feed on many species of trees, shrubs and low plants. Rhododendron is not native to Great Britain and it was not until it had become widely planted that the leafhopper became established here. Most leafhoppers feed on sap drawn from the vascular system of plants and leave no trace of their feeding sites, but a small group suck out the contents of the cells of leaves. Their presence is easily detected by the white mottling of empty cells on leaves where they are feeding. They are very small, and many have bold colour patterns which are best appreciated with a magnifying glass. They fly very readily when disturbed and several species have been found to be involved in spreading plant virus diseases.

The most fascinating life histories of any bugs are those of the aphids (greenfly, blackfly and their relatives). Aphids feed on the sap (not the leaf cells) of plants and it is thought that they are derived from an ancestral form of bug that fed on the sap of deciduous trees. The simplest forms are those that still live all the year round on deciduous trees and shrubs. Two common species with this type of life-cycle are the lime and sycamore aphids. Both can be a nuisance in car parks as they void the remains of their liquid meals as drops of a sweet, sticky fluid known as honeydew. This rain of honeydew, landing on vehicles parked beneath infested trees, gathers dust and makes unsightly spots of dirt on the bodywork.

In the autumn, male and female aphids mate and the female lays a few hard, cold-resistant eggs on the twigs before the onset of winter. The following spring, these eggs hatch into females which are wingless even as adults in most aphid species, and which give birth to active young, not eggs, without the intervention of males. There may then follow several generations of females, which are winged in the sycamore and lime aphids but either winged or wingless in other species. These all give birth to active young. In high summer, the sap of trees is low in nutrients and potential food is mostly locked up in leaf cells until the autumn. The lime and sycamore aphids spend this time of year as winged females resting quietly on the undersides of the leaves, and do not reproduce until the autumnal downward flow of sap commences. There is then another burst of reproductive activity, culminating in the birth of males and sexually reproducing females who will lay the over-wintering eggs.

Many aphid species have adopted the habit of migrating from their woody hosts to herbaceous plants during the summer months. They are then able to exploit the continuously high level of nutrients in these plants while the quality of sap is low. Two well-known examples of this life-style are the common blackfly of broad beans and the big greenfly that is often all too common on roses. We see the blackfly in the garden usually only on its herbaceous summer host, the bean plant, although it passes through a few generations in autumn and spring on the wild spindle tree, on which the over-wintering eggs are laid. In contrast, we usually see the greenfly on its woody host plant, the rose. For a period after flowering time, it migrates to wild scabious and teasel, presumably because these are more nutritious at that time of year. The autumn generations on the rose are usually less conspicuous than the spring ones.

APHIDS HAVE A host of natural enemies, including the adults and larvae of ladybirds and lacewings, and the larvae of hoverflies. In recent years insecticides have been developed which poison them but do not harm the useful predators which can move on to attack aphid colonies on other crops, where they may prevent them from multiplying to pest proportions. Often, some members of an aphid colony will be found on examination to be dead, dried-out, straw coloured husks. If leaves with these dead aphids on them are gathered and kept in plastic bags for a week or two, a variety of tiny wasps will emerge from the husks. These wasps have spent their larval lives as parasites inside the aphids, or sometimes as parasites of the parasites.

Many colonies of aphids will be found to be accompanied by ants.

At first glance, the ants appear to be wandering aimlessly about, clambering over the closely packed aphids without disturbing them. If a newly arrived ant is watched, however, the reason for its visit will become clear: it approaches several of the larger aphids from behind, touching them lightly with its antennae. Soon it finds one which responds by raising the hind end of its body from the leaf and exuding a drop of clear fluid honeydew, the remains of the plant sap from which the aphid has extracted some of the nutrients. It is still rich in sugars and the visiting ant quickly drinks the drop and moves on to another aphid, repeating the process until it is gorged. The abdomens of ants returning to their nests from an aphid colony are distinctly more swollen than those of their relatives on the outward journey. The sugary meal is then shared out in their nest and helps to fuel their frenetic activity, which contrasts markedly with the indolence of the aphids who are prepared to waste the sugars which are surplus to the requirements of their sedentary lives. The relationship between aphids and ants has been likened to that between cows and herdsmen and the ants, like good herdsmen, protect their charges from predators.

ONE OF THE MOST familiar of the natural groups of beetles is the ladybird family. The seven-spot and the smaller two-spot ladybird are both very frequent garden insects, although their abundance varies from year to year, and a good year for one is not necessarily a good year for both. In some years, immense numbers of ladybirds migrate in swarms and may even fly across the English Channel from the Continent, settling on the first beach they come to in a moving carpet or, if they fail to make the distance, their bodies may be washed up in huge numbers along the strand line. Their bright colours, daytime activity and indifference to being observed, all indicate that they are not good to eat, and insect-eating birds leave them alone. The reason for this becomes apparent if a ladybird is roughly handled: severe disturbance provokes the reaction called 'reflex bleeding' in which an evil-smelling, evil-tasting fluid is exuded through specially modified areas of the joints in the cuticle, especially the leg joints.

The two-spot ladybird is very variable in its colour pattern. The two black spots may be enlarged, often so much that they coalesce and the red ground-colour of the wing-cases is reduced in area to small patches isolated in a black background. An extreme form has the red colour restricted to two small, oblong spots. It is not at all clear why this species should be so variable, especially as the colour patterns of most of its relatives are quite stable. The proportion of the darker forms present in the population seems to increase through summer and to decrease during winter. Over-wintering ladybirds are often found in large clusters in the eaves of garden sheds and beneath slabs of loose bark on the trunks of dead trees. Ladybird grubs are active creatures with three pairs of legs near the front end of the body and a tapering abdomen. Like the adults, they feed on small, soft-bodied and relatively

immobile insects, such as greenfly. Their transformation to
pupa and thence to adult follows the beetle cycle described
earlier in this chapter.

Ladybirds and their grubs are not very particular about the
kind of insect food that they will take but are fairly selective
about where they live. For example, two-spot and seven-spot
ladybirds are seldom found on coniferous trees but the eyed
ladybird, which resembles a large seven-spot in which each
dark spot is surrounded by a pale ring, lives on conifers and is
rarely encountered elsewhere.

Another family of unpleasantly flavoured, brightly coloured predators is the soldier beetle family. A well-known,
non-British member of this family is 'Spanish fly' whose
body contains a potent poison which causes blisters if
applied to the skin, and a variety of unpleasant symptoms if
swallowed. The oblong, red and black, soft-bodied beetles
which schoolchildren call 'bloodsuckers' belong to this
group. They abound in summer on flowering plants and
shrubs where they devour any unwary insect that comes
their way. Their carnivorous, velvety grubs live on the
ground and somewhat resemble
those of ladybirds.

A third group of predators are the ground beetles. Most species of this family are coloured in sombre blacks and browns and rely on their nocturnal habits to protect them from insect-eating birds. By day they hide away in secluded places in the upper layers of the soil or among dead leaves. A few minutes spent on the garden path or lawn after dark with a pocket torch will reveal a surprising abundance and variety of ground beetles scurrying about in search of their prey, especially on a warm, moist night.

The glow worm beetle is a specialized kind of predator. The grub feeds on snails and consequently glow worms are most frequently found in areas such as chalk downs, where snails abound. Adult glow worms do not live very long and it is thought that they may not feed at all. The grub has a pair of luminous spots on the underside of the body near the hind end. The female glow worm closely resembles the grub, lacking both wings and wing cases. The male is rather like a brown soldier beetle. Both sexes have a large luminous area on the underside of the body which can be seen from a considerable distance in the dark. Males fly readily at night, seeking out the females by sight. The glow worm is one of very few luminous animals in Britain and it is worth leaving an area of rough grass undisturbed in a chalky garden if these intriguing insects are known to be present in the neighbourhood.

A great many rove beetles are also predators, though many species of this huge family feed on decaying plant material and fungi. Most have greatly shortened wing cases like those of earwigs, and the wings are folded in a very complex way to get them stowed away in such a small space. The processes of folding and unfolding the wings can be watched if a rove beetle in the mood for flight is kept under observation. If allowed to climb to the top of a grass blade or a finger, it will raise its cases and the wings will spring out. If it is then shaken down before it has the opportunity to fly away it will tuck the wings away again.

One of the largest of the rove beetles is the entirely black devil's coach horse. When disturbed, this beetle lifts its head with the jaws

Beetles are the most numerous of all insect species; a few interesting and eye-catching kinds are shown here. The wasp beetle (top left) is a harmless and probably quite tasty insect that mimics the yellow and black uniform and jerky movements of a wasp to protect itself from predators. Click beetles (bottom left) may drop to the ground when alarmed. If one lands on its back, it bends its body backwards until resting on head and tail tip, then suddenly lets go, springing upwards with a click. The male stag beetle, with his huge, antler-like jaws, is the giant among British beetles. The big larvae live for several years in rotting stumps; adults fly at dusk on sultry nights. The rove beetle or cocktail beetle (climbing a grass stem) has short wing cases but well developed wings; it can run fast and take off quickly. Its larger, all-black relative, the devil's coach-horse (on tree root), is very fierce and can give a sharp bite. When alarmed it opens its jaws, raises its tail over its back, and spurts a strong-smelling vapour in a very effective defensive display. The seven-spot and two-spot ladybirds (right) are popular beetles, well-known for the good they and their larvae do in devouring aphids. Their bright and boldly-contrasting colours warn birds and other would-be predators that they are distasteful.

Most leaf beetles enjoy the sunshine and feed openly by day on the foliage of plants. Many are rounded in shape, smooth, and metallic in colouring. The conspicuous adults and larvae of the Colorado beetle (left) are so striking in appearance that they are immediately recognizable. This is a very serious pest of potato fields in its native Rocky Mountains in North America. Occasionally it makes its way to Britain; anyone finding it must notify the Ministry of Agriculture at once, so that the beetle is not given a chance to multiply and establish itself as a serious pest here. Asparagus beetles (top right), with their larvae live and feed on the fern of asparagus plants. Flea beetles (bottom right) are very small and very numerous beetles that jump with their hind legs which have thickened thighs. Some, such as the turnip flea beetle and the potato flea beetle, are very destructive and do great damage to crops.

open and cocks its abdomen upwards, which gives it a threatening appearance. The flexibility of their bodies means that rove beetles can penetrate places that are inaccessible to beetles of a more conventional shape. For this reason they are often abundant in such habitats as compost heaps and piles of grass cuttings.

When digging the vegetable patch it is not unusual to come across long, shiny, flexible, cylindrical grubs with a hard, straw-coloured cuticle. These are wireworms and they can be very destructive. The most obvious damage that they do is to make small holes in potatoes and carrots, but they do much more by eating the fine, fibrous roots of all manner of plants, reducing their vigour. It takes several years for a wireworm to become full-grown, at which time it moults to become a pupa, a few inches below the surface of the soil. In a few weeks, the pupa in turn moults to give rise to an adult click beetle. Click beetles are long, hard, shiny and short-legged, usually black or various shades of brown in colour. If it is turned over on to its back, a click beetle will attempt to right itself by flexing slightly at a joint roughly in the middle of its body and then suddenly snapping the two halves in the opposite direction. This operation produces, in the larger species at least, an audible click and shoots the insect into the air when, with luck, it will fall the right way up or among vegetation which it can grip with its legs and so right itself.

A DIFFERENT KIND OF subterranean, root-eating beetle grub is the cockchafer, a fat, pale, soft-bodied creature, usually found with its body curled into a characteristic C-shape. Like the wireworm, it feeds underground for several years before pupating. The adult beetle, which emerges from the soil in late April or May, is sometimes known as the may bug. Several small relatives with similar life-histories are also found in gardens. One is the beautiful, golden-green rose chafer, which may cause annoyance by eating the petals of flowers, especially of roses.

A near relation of the chafer is the stag beetle. This, the largest of all British beetles, also has a life history similar to that of the chafers but the grubs feed on damp, rotten wood, usually below ground. A large, old tree stump left to decay instead of being dug out may well become the home of a colony of stag beetle grubs and, in due course, the owner of the garden may be rewarded on warm summer evenings by the sight of these majestic insects flying slowly about.

Many other beetles play a role in breaking down dead wood and bark. Some, like the longhorn beetles, attack living trees and their grubs burrow deep into the wood, even killing the tree in the case of a severe infestation. A common species in gardens, usually doing little serious damage, is the wasp beetle, so named because the yellow stripes across its black wing cases resemble those of a wasp.

It is not only dead wood and other plant remains that are used by beetles. Various species perform the function of clearing up the dead bodies of larger animals. The best known of these are the burying beetles, of which there are several species, some clad entirely in funeral black and others with bold, orange patches on their wing cases. If two or three come across the body of a mouse or a small bird, they excavate the soil from beneath it until it sinks into the hole and is buried. They then lay their eggs on it and the grubs feed on the interred remains. The burial of the little corpse presumably serves the function of concealing it from foxes, blowflies and the numerous other creatures on the lookout for fresh or not so fresh meat.

There are two large groups of beetles which feed mainly on the living tissues of green plants: leaf beetles and weevils. Seedling cabbages, turnips and radishes often have their leaves riddled with tiny holes by flea beetles, tiny leaf beetles which are able to jump. They are all oval in shape, very small and may be black all over, with or without a blue, green or bronze metallic sheen, or they may be black with a broad, yellow stripe along each wing case. The grubs of most flea beetles feed on the roots of the plants, but those of the turnip flea live between the upper and lower surfaces of the leaves, making a leaf-mine like those caused by the maggots of certain flies or the caterpillars of some small moths. Many leaf beetle grubs live in the open on the foliage of their host plants, together with the adult beetles. One such species is the asparagus beetle, adults and grubs of which often damage the 'fern' of asparagus in late summer. An even less welcome species in the garden is the Colorado beetle, whose black and yellow striped adults and red grubs are very destructive to potato crops. Intensive publicity and eradication campaigns have so far prevented this beetle

Weevils are plant-eating beetles whose heads are drawn out into a characteristic snout or rostrum which varies in length and shape from species to species, but is longer in the female. The antennae, part way down the snout, are clubbed and have an elbow at the end of the long first joint so that the weevil can tuck them neatly against the snout when it goes to rest. The female of the nut weevil has a very long down-curved snout. She uses this to bore a hole through the soft shell of a young hazelnut into the kernel and there lays a single egg which she inserts by means of a long extensible ovipositor. The grub that hatches from this egg stays inside the shell feeding and growing until the nut falls from the tree in the autumn. The grub then gnaws its way out of the shell and burrows into the earth where it pupates and hibernates. In the spring the adult weevils hatch from their pupal skins underground and appear on the trees when the hazels come into leaf.

from becoming a permanent feature of the British agricultural scene.

If the garden is large enough to allow a patch of rough vegetation to grow up, with perennial weeds in it, the variety of plant-feeding beetles will be greatly increased. One likely addition will be the green tortoise beetle, also a member of the leaf beetle group. The adults are rather like green ladybirds. Only the tips of their black feet and their short antennae can be seen from above, the head is completely concealed from view. Both the adults and the black, spiny grubs live on thistles.

The leaflets of pea and bean plants are often found with semi-circular nicks in the edges. These are caused by the activities of pea weevils, which bite the edges of the leaflets while they are still folded in bud. Pea weevil grubs feed on the roots of the pea and bean plants but are not usually serious pests. The pea weevil, like all weevils, bears its jaws at the tip of a snout-like prolongation of the head. In this species it is short and broad, but in its relative, the nut weevil, the snout is slender and almost as long as the body. Nut weevil grubs live in the kernels of hazelnuts. The female weevil bores a hole deep into the nut she has chosen with the tiny jaws at the apex of her slender snout, and then introduces the egg into it by means of her long, retractable ovipositor. The business of drilling the hole and laying the egg is extremely laborious and time-consuming but, with patience, the human observer can witness the whole of the process, and many other aspects of insect biology, thus adding enormously to the enjoyment of nature within the garden.

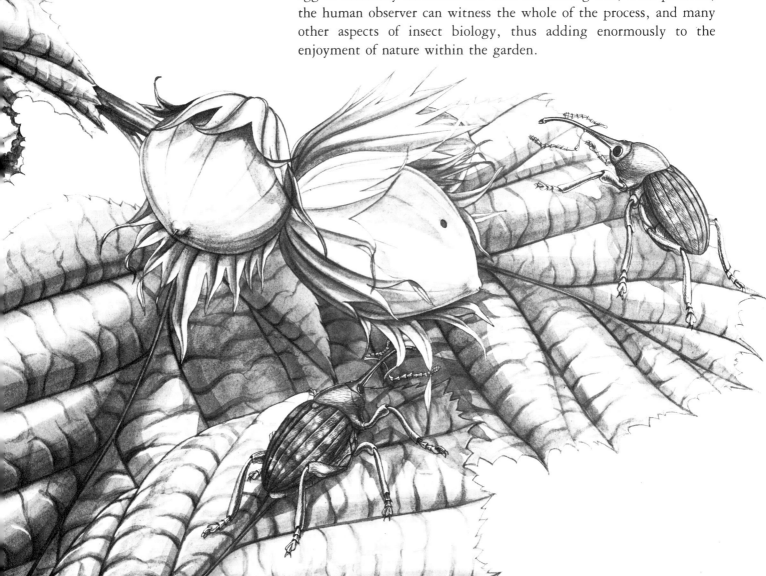

Spiders and Flies

Flies and spiders were associated in people's minds long before the word 'fly' had any precise entomological meaning. But a large proportion of the victims of spiders are members of the order *Diptera*, which are the flies of this chapter, so the relationship is still a valid one. We will look at them first before discussing spiders.

The *Diptera*, or two-winged flies, are distinguished by having only one pair of wings, which correspond to the fore-wings of other insects. The hind-wings have been transformed, in the course of evolution, to a pair of small clubbed stalks called halteres, which vibrate in phase with the wings and serve to control the flight. The wing-beat, which determines the speed of vibration, is very rapid, especially in the smaller flies such as mosquitoes where they complete an up-and-down stroke 500 or more times in a second. The figure for the house-fly is about 200, and a tiny midge has been shown to beat its wings at a rate of more than 1000 times a second. This is not quite so incredible as it might seem, when one considers how minute are the distances that the wing tips actually travel as they beat up and down.

An entomologist specializing in flies is called a dipterist. If a person so qualified collected flies throughout the summer in a country garden, he would certainly end up with several hundred species, for over 5000 different types of flies have been collected and identified in the British Isles, and a few more are added every year. But most of the flies in your garden are so small that they escape the notice of a casual observer, or are so similar to one another that meticulous counting of bristles and measuring of leg joints is needed to separate the species. Nevertheless, anyone who gives them some attention will soon realize that flies are present in the garden in great diversity.

Taken as a whole, the *Diptera* are among the least likeable of insects. Many carry disease: the 'ague' that plagued the human inhabitants of marshy districts in England a couple of centuries ago was malaria. It was thought then to be due to the bad air of the marshes but, in fact, it was contracted from the bite of mosquitoes. The disease has gone from this country now, but the bites of these and other flies remain as irritant's. House-flies and bluebottles buzz maddeningly round our heads and breed disgustingly in food carelessly exposed.

It is a relief to turn away from *Diptera* to a group of flies that offer us

In the late summer the flowers of Michaelmas daisies are visited by several kinds of yellow and black striped flies known as hover-flies or flower-flies. The males may be seen hovering near the flowers while waiting for the females. They feed on nectar or pollen, but their blind, transparent white or green larvae are carnivorous and feed on aphids. A larva pierces a greenfly with its hooked mouth, holds it up, like a seal balancing a ball, and when it is sucked dry, bends backwards leaving the empty skin behind it. A single larva may eat fifty greenfly in a day. Syrphus balteatus *(top) is on the wing all year, though commonest in summer;* S.ribesii *(below) flies from April until November.*

neither danger, discomfort nor offence, but are pretty and harmless, and even beneficial. These are the hoverflies, which are lovers of flowers and present in summer around the shrubs and herbaceous borders of every garden. They are well named, for their most remarkable feature is their wonderfully controlled flight. You will often see a hoverfly poised apparently motionless in the air like a tiny helicopter. If you make a movement it will dart away, but if you wait quietly it is very likely to return and hover in just the same position as before. It is doing far more than simply standing still in the air, for the air out of doors, even on the most sultry day, is never still; there is always some lateral drift as well as eddies caused by rising air currents and the passage of the breeze round leaves and branches. How, then, does the fly avoid being constantly carried up and down, to and fro?

Almost certainly it maintains its position by means of its sense of sight. The compound eyes of insects are less efficient than ours at forming images, but very sensitive to slight movements. The smallest shift in the fly's position relative to its surroundings is instantly perceived and is instantly corrected by a minute but exact adjustment in the action of the wings. And so it remains motionless in relation, not to the air which sustains it, but to noticeable objects in its field of vision. Both hoverflies and dragonflies (which are not *Diptera*) have unusually large compound eyes. The dragonflies need acute vision for hunting and capturing other insects in flight; the hoverflies need it for precise control of their hovering. All of them feed by settling on flowers and sucking up the nectar.

Another attractive feature of hoverflies is their bright coloration and pattern. Many of them are striped with yellow, red or white against a background of black, and in this resemble wasps. Some of the larger ones do indeed look very like wasps, and it is generally supposed that this is a case of mimicry, the hoverflies deriving protection from birds and other predators by their resemblance to insects with formidable stings, which the birds learn to avoid. But this does not apply to some of the smaller species which, if they resemble wasps at all, resemble small ones which cannot sting effectively in defence. It is quite possible that the bright and distinctive colours are simply recognitional, as those of butterflies are believed to be.

There is one kind of hoverfly—the drone-fly—that does seem to be a mimic of a stinging insect, the honeybee. Very common in gardens, it is brown and hairy, and about the size of a bee. Few people who are not naturalists will pick a drone-fly off a window pane with their bare fingers. It is quite likely that it deceives birds, and it certainly confused mankind for 2000 years or more. This fly is the origin of the persistent myth that an animal carcass, left to putrefy, will generate a swarm of bees that can be expected to produce honey. It is encountered in the Old Testament story of Samson and the lion, and his famous riddle: 'Out of the strong came forth sweetness.' Samson had killed a lion and left it to rot, and the people of his time firmly believed that a swarm of honeybees would emerge from it. The 'bees' were, in fact, drone-flies, whose larvae feed, grow and pupate in any sort of liquid rottenness.

Drone-flies are often abundant on Michaelmas daisies and ivy bloom in the autumn. Although they look rather like honeybees, their way of sitting and walking is different and, of course, the single pair of wings immediately distinguishes them. The larvae of the drone-fly, known as rat-tailed maggots, can be found not only in decaying carcasses but in any stagnant and heavily contaminated water; seepages from manure heaps are specially favoured. The larva is about 2.5 centimetres (1 inch) long and has an elongated and extensible tail which serves as a breathing siphon. It can be shortened or lengthened so that it just reaches the surface of the water up to 15 centimetres (6 inches) deep.

Not all hoverfly larvae live in this way. I mentioned earlier that these flies can be beneficial in gardens. In fact, as larvae they feed on aphids or greenfly—most of the prettily marked flower-loving hoverflies have larvae with this mode of feeding. They are elongate, without legs and taper towards the front end, and you should learn to recognize them and distinguish them from caterpillars when you find them on rose bushes. If you watch one for a few minutes, you may see it seize an unhappy aphid and hold it aloft, to give its struggles no purchase, while it sucks out the contents of its body. The flies themselves are also beneficial as pollinators of flowers of all kinds.

There is one black sheep among the hoverflies,

The large brown hover-fly Eristalis tenax *is called the drone-fly from its remarkable resemblance to the male, or drone, honey-bee. Male drone-flies hover in open spaces, and both sexes feed on the nectar and pollen of flowers such as hogweed. Their larvae live in water and are known as rat-tailed maggots from the long breathing tube which extends from their tails to the water surface. These flies may be seen in early spring feeding at crocuses and dandelion flowers.*

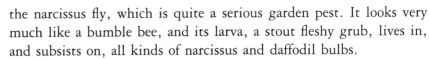

the narcissus fly, which is quite a serious garden pest. It looks very much like a bumble bee, and its larva, a stout fleshy grub, lives in, and subsists on, all kinds of narcissus and daffodil bulbs.

To identify all the hoverflies you see visiting your flowers you would need to make a close study of the breed, but a few of the commonest ones are fairly easy to recognize, though they have never been given English names. *Syrphus balteatus* can be very abundant, and is a small, slender fly with an orange body and alternating broad and narrow transverse black stripes. *Syrphus ribesii* is almost as common, about the same size but stouter, and has a rather wasplike pattern of broad black and yellow bars. *Catabomba pyrastri* is a large, handsome hoverfly, black with three white crescent-shaped marks on each side of the body.

S O MUCH FOR the hoverflies. Another easily recognizable garden species is St Mark's fly which appears quite early in the spring, about the date of St Mark's day. It is a sluggish black hairy fly, as long as a blue-bottle but not so stout, and is a common sight in April and early May, sitting about on leaves.

In summer the whole countryside, gardens included, is often invaded by swarms of daddy-long-legs or crane-flies. If you watch your lawn closely at such a time, you may

see the big clumsy flies emerging from their pupae in the turf, or at any rate you will find the papery brown pupa cases that they have vacated. Their larvae are the unattractive grey grubs called leatherjackets which feed on the roots of all kinds of plants, and damage lawns and cultivated plants alike. The starlings that walk and run about on the lawn, constantly probing the turf with their beaks, devour great numbers of leatherjackets, for which we have reason to be thankful to them. The commonest daddy-long-legs is a large plain brown one, *Tipula paludosa*, but in gardens one often encounters a smaller species clearly marked with yellow and black. This is *Nephrotoma maculata*, and its larva, also a root-feeder, is sometimes a garden pest of some importance.

At almost any time of the year, but especially in the autumn, one may see dancing swarms of gnats or midges that hover and rise and fall, but constantly maintain their position in one place. These are not mosquitoes but harmless gnats of a family of *Diptera* known to entomologists as *Chironomidae*. The larva of one of them, *Chironomus plumosus*, is the creature known as a bloodworm, a little wriggling red worm found in any stagnant water, including rainwater butts.

Far more common in water butts and small garden ponds are the larvae of mosquitoes. These often swarm in the water collected from the roof and more or less contaminated by decaying leaves and bird droppings. They are small, colourless creatures that swim with a curious somersaulting action and float on the surface of the water to obtain air for respiration. The pupa looks like a little dark-coloured seed and it also swims actively, a very unusual thing for a pupa to do. The commonest mosquito with this habit of breeding is *Culex pipiens*; the Latin name refers to the shrill piping 'ping' made by its wings, beating at around 500 times a second. The eggs are laid in little raft-like batches on the surface of the water. As is well known, only female mosquitoes 'bite'; the males do not take meals of blood but feed mostly on the nectar of flowers. Most fortunately, the female of *Culex pipiens* does not attack humans but apparently confines itself to birds. However, there is another, larger, mosquito that also breeds in water butts in comparatively small numbers, which does attack humans. *Theobaldia annulata* has spotted wings and white-ringed legs and body, and is a savage brute. The females come into houses in the autumn to hibernate and are difficult to locate by day, but at night they fly from time to time and sustain themselves with the blood of people sleeping, or trying to sleep, in the dark.

Crane-flies have long thin bodies, narrow wings and such long slender legs that they are also known as 'daddy-long-legs'. There are nearly three hundred different species in Britain, and the largest of them has the greatest wingspan of all British flies. One of the commonest is Tipula paludosa, *a large plain brown insect found among grass and weeds in meadows and the less cultivated corners of gardens. Adult crane-flies generally fly at night, but during the day can readily be disturbed from the long grass where they are hiding: they fly with characteristic dancing flight, their long legs dangling. Crane-fly larvae live in the soil; they are greyish-brown grubs with tough skins and are commonly known as 'leatherjackets'. They are serious pests as they feed on the roots of grasses and other plants, working just below the surface of the soil by day and above it at night. They continue feeding right through the autumn, winter and spring until, when fully grown, they pupate in late spring or early summer. About two weeks later the slim, horned pupae push their way half out of the soil for the adult crane-flies to emerge. The females continue the cycle by laying hundreds of small black eggs in the soil, depositing them in the earth with their long pointed ovipositors. Leatherjackets and daddy-long-legs are eaten in large numbers by rooks, gulls and lapwings on farmland, and by starlings, blackbirds, spotted flycatchers and other insect-eaters, such as hedgehogs, in our gardens. Nonetheless, enough usually survive to be a serious nuisance. Only a summer of prolonged hot sunshine and drying winds can significantly reduce the numbers of these insects, since the damp cool conditions of a typical British summer is what crane-flies flourish best in.*

After a strong wind has destroyed their webs, garden spiders have to rebuild them before they can catch another meal. The construction follows a set pattern. The first stage is to bridge the gap between two main supports. The spider either pays out a thread of silk which floats in the air and catches on, or it drops down, walks across and up the next support, pulling the thread behind it.

When the first strand is solid, a loose thread is passed across and, by hanging from the middle, the spider pulls it into a V which will become the centre of the web. More spokes are added to make a firm foundation. Then the spider lays down a spiral of dry silk and, using this as a foothold, pays out a new spiral of sticky silk, eating the first spiral as it goes. The silk is placed accurately by the legs so that the finished spiral is beautifully even.

Evenings in the garden are sometimes made miserable by very small biting midges on which entomologists have bestowed the jaw-breaking family name *Ceratopogonidae*, meaning 'horny-bearded', though there scarcely seems to be room for an adornment of this kind on such a minute insect. Here again, only the females bite, and it is surprising that they can pierce human skin. The bite of these midges and mosquitoes causes irritation because, before sucking up their meal of blood, the insects inject an anticoagulant to prevent the blood from clotting and blocking their hair-fine proboscis. The substance injected is also poisonous and causes swelling and irritation around the wound. Let us turn away from flies and consider their deadly enemies, the spiders.

AN EMINENT AUTHORITY on spiders has maintained that insects 'learned' to fly, in the evolutionary sense, in order to escape from spiders. Certainly both were in existence over 350 million years ago when the insects had no other effective enemies, and the spiders of the time were probably simple hunters without the wonderful web-spinning skills of their modern descendants.

Spiders are not insects. The most obvious difference between them lies in the number of legs, six in insects, eight in spiders. An insect's body is divided into three parts, the head, the thorax or chest and the abdomen. In spiders the head and thorax are united to form the forepart of the body, behind which the abdomen, distinctly separated, forms the remainder. Finally, most insects have wings, spiders never do.

All spiders are predators: there is no such thing as a herbivorous spider, and all kill their prey with a poisonous bite delivered by a pair of sharp hollow fangs under the head. Some spiders of other countries can pierce human skin with their fangs and their venom may produce severe or occasionally dangerous symptoms. No British species can do this and there is no need to be afraid of them. They have a peculiar method of feeding: they bite their victims repeatedly and inject digestive juices into the wounds, then suck back the liquid so produced, going on in this way until only empty skins or shells remain.

Another universal feature of spiders is their ability to spin silken threads from special organs called spinnerets on the hind end of the abdomen. The predominant sense of most spiders is not that of sight or hearing or smell, but of perception of tension of threads of their own spinning. Wherever it goes a spider trails a silken thread along which it can retrace its path, and in its own web or silk-lined burrow it finds its way about by its sense of touch. They make cocoons of silk to enclose and protect their eggs, and wrap their victims in parcels of silk. Very small spiders travel by becoming airborne on long strands of silk paid out from their spinnerets for the purpose.

The most remarkable silken structure is the familiar wheel-shaped orb-web. Very briefly, this is how it is made. Firstly, the spider pays out a thread which is carried by the air across a suitable space and becomes entangled in something on the far side of it. It is strong enough to allow the spider to walk across and strengthen it with extra threads; this is called the bridge line. She then drops from a central point on it to a twig or similar object below, trailing a thread behind her. By repeated dropping and climbing, she constructs a frame in which the radii or spokes are next disposed. She walks along each one of these to make the next one, and the angles between the radii at the centre are constant, though the spaces between their ends are varied because the frame is not a circle; a remarkable exercise in unconscious geometry. Next, the central platform is made, and then the spider walks round and round laying down a spiral thread of silk from near the centre to the outside of the web, but this is a temporary structure. Finally, she walks round this spiral again, destroying it as she goes, and replacing it with a spiral of special silk covered with minute droplets of sticky fluid. The web is now complete and any insect that touches it sticks to it and, in struggling, becomes more entangled.

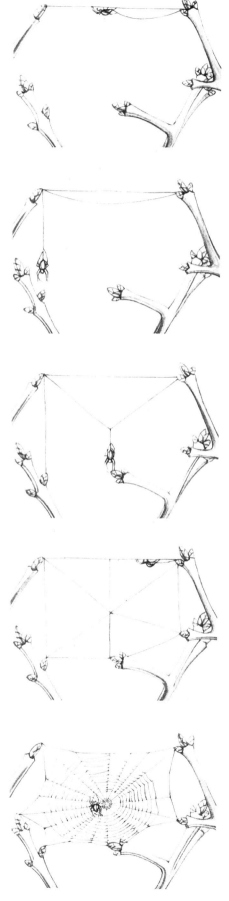

To GET AN IDEA of how numerous spiders are in your garden, go out soon after dawn on a foggy or misty morning in October. The webs, normally almost invisible, are all shining white with minute droplets of water, and they are everywhere, overhead and underfoot, on bushes and fences, and adorning angles and projections all round the house. The form of many of them is a good guide to the identity of the spiders that made them.

Some of the orb-webs will be those of the garden spider whose method of web-making has been described above. These webs are large with a closely netted platform in the middle and the spirals coming quite close to it. When the spider is present it sits head downwards on the platform. It is a fat heavy female, brown or yellowish with a pattern of white spots often arranged in the form of a cross, and it is fully grown by about August. At this time the much more slender males wander about in search of females to mate with. Having found a tenanted web, the male spider advances cautiously and plucks at it, and at first always meets with a fierce attack which he evades by swinging clear on his own thread. But he is persistent and returns again and again and, at last, if he is lucky, she accepts him as a mate rather than a meal, and mating takes place. This is in a mode peculiar to spiders: the male has previously transferred some of his sperm into his palps, organs on each side of his head that work like a pair of tiny hollowed-out hands. With these he injects the sperm into the body of the female.

In September or October the female leaves her web and lays a mass of several hundred yellow eggs in a crevice or under loose bark, and encloses them in a cocoon of yellow silk. Her bulk is now greatly reduced and she remains beside the eggs for a few weeks, then dies. The eggs hatch during warm spells of weather in May, and the tiny black and yellow spiders go outside where they form a tight ball or

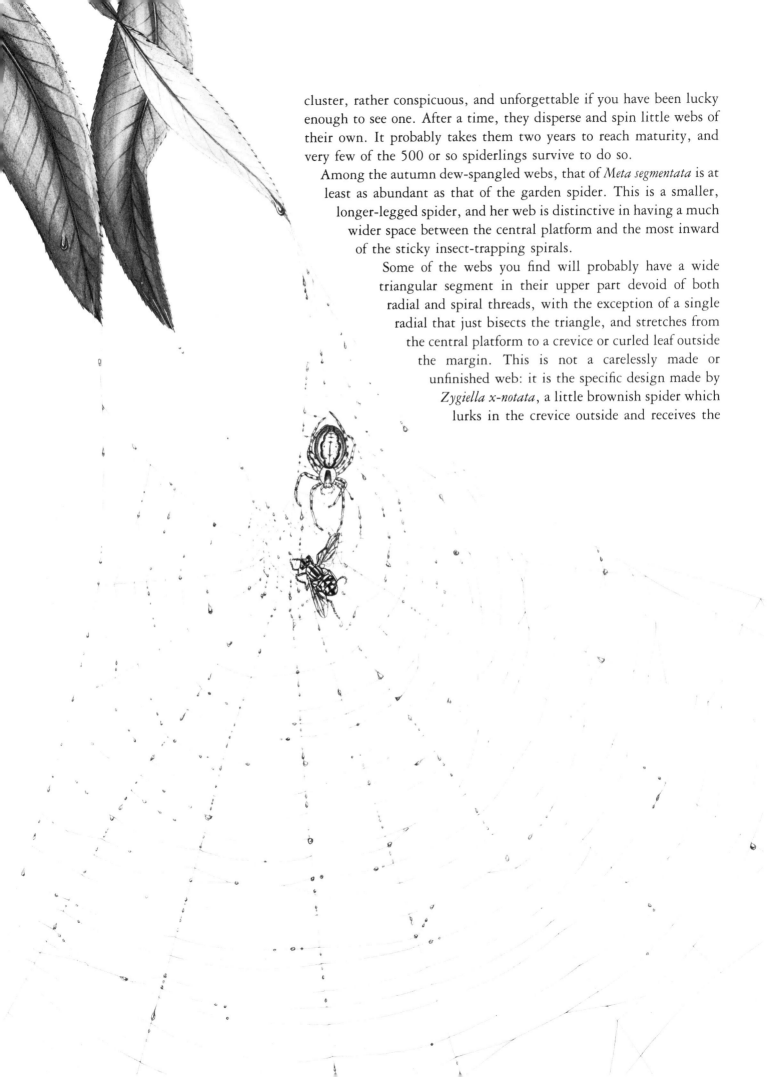

cluster, rather conspicuous, and unforgettable if you have been lucky enough to see one. After a time, they disperse and spin little webs of their own. It probably takes them two years to reach maturity, and very few of the 500 or so spiderlings survive to do so.

Among the autumn dew-spangled webs, that of *Meta segmentata* is at least as abundant as that of the garden spider. This is a smaller, longer-legged spider, and her web is distinctive in having a much wider space between the central platform and the most inward of the sticky insect-trapping spirals.

Some of the webs you find will probably have a wide triangular segment in their upper part devoid of both radial and spiral threads, with the exception of a single radial that just bisects the triangle, and stretches from the central platform to a crevice or curled leaf outside the margin. This is not a carelessly made or unfinished web: it is the specific design made by *Zygiella x-notata*, a little brownish spider which lurks in the crevice outside and receives the message that a victim is struggling in the net below her through vibrations in that single radial thread.

The little spiders that appear from nowhere, running on your sleeve, are often called money spiders because they are believed to bring good luck. There are about 250 species of them found in Britain, and only an experienced arachnologist can attempt to identify them. Arachne, by the way, was a maiden in Greek mythology who unwisely challenged the goddess Athene to a contest in weaving, and won it. This so annoyed the goddess that she most unsportingly turned the poor girl into a spider. Hence 'Arachnida', the group of animals in which spiders are classified, and other scientific terms relating to them. But to return to the money spiders.

You are likely to overlook them altogether except on misty autumnal mornings, when their webs, which consist of irregular horizontal sheets of closely woven silk, are conspicuous. The large ones are called 'hammock webs' and are often spun near the base of hedges. In these, there are vertical threads below the web that anchor it to the ground, plucking little pointed projections down from its under surface. There is also an open tangle of threads above the sheet. Small webs of the same kind can be found, picked out by the dew, all over the lawn and in any low-growing herbage. The little spiders subsist by catching small insects that fall accidentally on to the sheet.

There are three British species of Zygiella *spiders. They all spin the same distinctive pattern of orb web in which one of the strands radiating from the centre is isolated instead of being joined to the sticky spirals as in the webs of other orb-builders. The webs of* Zygiella *therefore look incomplete and badly made, but the isolated thread is left unconnected to the rest of the web for a specific purpose: it acts as a very sensitive communication cord between the spider and its prey.*

Zygiella *does not lie in wait in the hub of her web as do other orb-spiders, but hides in a silken retreat near the web. To this retreat stretches the isolated radial line, and the spider waits, one foot resting on the thread. As soon as a fly or other insect blunders into the web, its frantic vibrations as it struggles to free itself are transmitted to the waiting spider who rushes out on to the web, locates the prey and captures it with her fangs. Her bite poisons and subdues the fly, which she then wraps in silk and carries to her lair to be consumed at leisure.*

Zebra spiders are jumping spiders: they stalk their prey, cat-like, with slow deliberation and capture it by leaping upon it at the last moment. Two of their eight eyes are conspicuously large and forwardly directed, and provide acute vision in bright light. Should a zebra spider miss its prey and fall, it will be saved by the thread of silk anchored to the point of take-off. In spring the brightly patterned male jumping spider performs an elaborate courtship dance in front of the drabber female: she watches intently as he zig-zags on tiptoe, his front legs extended as if to mesmerise her. After mating, the eggs are laid in a silk cocoon in a cranny or crevice and guarded by the female.

It is these tiny spiders, and perhaps the young of some larger ones, that disperse themselves on the wind in their thousands. The spider climbs to the top of a bush or tall stem and pays out a silk thread into the air. As this grows longer and longer the spider's situation becomes like that of a very small boy flying a very large kite in a hurricane. It lets go and becomes airborne, and may travel a few yards to a nearby tree or may embark on a journey of hundreds of miles. When very large numbers behave in this way, the countryside becomes covered with a thin mantle of closely inter-crossing silk lines; called gossamer.

THERE ARE PLENTY of spiders that do not use their silk to spin webs at all, but hunt their prey as lions and wolves do. One group is appropriately called the *Lycosidae*, or wolf spiders. They run actively on the ground and are frequently seen on paths and flower beds. The females enclose their eggs in a round white cocoon, which they drag about attached to their spinnerets, and mother wolf spiders are easily recognized by this conspicuous egg-bag. When the young spiders hatch they spend a few days riding clustered together on the mother's back, giving her the appearance of being infested with parasites. Wolf spiders hunt their prey by sight and form an exception to the rule that spiders have thread tension as their dominant sense.

There are lots more spiders to be met with in your garden, but the last one I have space to mention is the zebra spider, much smaller than a wolf spider but a ferocious hunter with large, efficient, forward-looking eyes. It is a little black and white spider that runs about with quick jerky movements on walls and around windows, and in summer often finds its way into the house. It is pleasant to watch it stalk a fly, when it behaves exactly like a cat after a bird. As it approaches, its advance becomes more and more cautious until it is near enough to make a final spring. If the hunt has been on a vertical surface both will generally fall towards the ground, but they do not fall far for, as it leaps, the spider anchors a thread which soon arrests their fall like a mountaineer's rope.

Occasionally a zebra spider will stalk a fly on the wrong side of a window pane. When she makes her final leap, her astonishment and indignation as she scrabbles at the glass, and the complete unconcern of the fly, combine to make this a richly ludicrous performance.

Worms, Snails and Slugs

Although worms are quite different from slugs and snails, the three are often grouped together, probably because they all possess soft bodies and slimy skins. They have little else in common, however. Even the name 'worm' causes some confusion, as it is used to describe a host of unrelated animals, including parasitic flukes and tapeworms in addition to the more obvious white roundworms or nematodes. Members of this last group are found living almost everywhere; in animals and plants as well as moving freely in the soil. Although many nematodes are quite harmless, a number do cause diseases in plants and animals. None of these parasites is a close relative of the helpful earthworm, although there is often some confusion of identity between them. Slugs and snails have a quite different reputation—hardly anyone has a good word to say for them. We shall be considering how much damage they do later, but it is impossible not to remark that our opinion of them is governed mainly by their feel and appearance.

Slugs and snails belong to a large group of animals called molluscs, most of which live in the sea. There, many of them, such as the octopus, can move quickly; others—for example, the sea slugs—have a complexity of form which, together with their colouring, gives them a breath-taking beauty. Marine molluscs can be fast and shapely because their bodies are supported by the water; their relatives on land, on the other hand, are limited to a simple contour and to crawling about. Land slugs and snails do have one marvellous specialization, however—a simple lung. A garden slug breathes through a respiratory opening found on the smooth, rounded, cape-like area behind the head. From time to time, this huge 'nostril' is closed, especially if the slug is disturbed. Some, such as the large black and large red varieties, are an attractive colour, and inquisitive children are often tempted to touch them only to recoil at their slimy feel and firm muscular contractions. Such contractions are merely a demonstration of the slug's defence mechanisms at work; they have saved many of them from being eaten by potential predators. These protective devices are only one aspect of a fascinating way of life, and it would certainly be a shame if they prevented us from getting to know the creatures better. I know several people who have kept slugs as pets and one young lady, not a naturalist, who thoroughly recommends them.

Although there are many different species of earthworm, they are all basically similar. Their shape equips them to burrow through the soil: an activity which is very helpful to the gardener because it improves aeration and drainage. Although other animals, such as eels and snakes, have the same shape and can burrow, too, they do not tunnel in the same special way. An earthworm alters the shape of its segments so that several adjacent ones expand simultaneously against the wall of the burrow, while another group is extending forwards. The worm moves as waves of contraction and extension pass along its body. To help anchor itself, it has rows of spear-like setae which it can dig into the soil, and which are retracted into its body when not in use. These setae are exceptionally strong—as we have probably all discovered at one time or another when we have tried to pull a worm out of its burrow. As a worm moves it makes use of existing crevices in the soil, which it finds by using its sensitive prostomium. From above, this looks like its first small segment, but is more likely a fleshy nose hanging above the mouth. It seems amazing that animals with such soft bodies can burrow in quite heavy soil, but it has been calculated that a worm can exert a force of 1 kilogram to 1 square centimetre ($2\frac{1}{4}$ pounds to $\frac{1}{8}$ square inch) against the ground. Thank goodness all that work is not being used against us!

WORMS ALSO IMPROVE the soil when they feed. As they move, they can suck earth in through their mouths to their gizzards, where a churning action grinds the vegetable fragments against sandy particles in the soil. Some organic material is digested and absorbed as the soil passes through the worm, but there is still a lot left in the casts which leave the animal's body. The casts are easily broken down to humus by the soil bacteria and so the soil is enriched. A worm might eat a quarter of its own weight in soil every day, and there can be up to 850 worms in a square metre of soil, so a great deal can be treated in this way. Only a few, including the long worm, *Aubophora longa*, leave their casts on the surface (most others produce them just below), but they all help in mixing the soil and bringing nutrients to the surface. Each year, worms are capable of leaving a layer of soil at the surface which is between 1 millimetre ($\frac{1}{25}$ inch) and 5 centimetres (2 inches) thick.

Earthworms can also feed on decaying leaves which they collect from the surface. They usually grasp these by the tip and pull them down into their burrows, where they can be eaten in greater safety and kept in store for times when surface feeding is impossible.

Lumbricus terrestris, the common garden worm, feeds in this way, too, and the entrance to its burrow is often found plugged with leaves. If the plug is removed the worm will soon replace it, and if leaves are unavailable, a 'worm cairn' of small stones may cover the entrance instead. Some worms feed mainly on leaves and so, for most of the time, do not have to tunnel to feed. Their burrows are much less extensive than those of soil-feeding species. Worms therefore, play an important role in helping to break down the leaves that fall each year

and in making foods available for future plant growth.

Another important way in which earthworms assist the gardener is in the formation of aggregates, groups of soil particles which are cemented together in a way that aids drainage and aeration. Soils with better aggregates can hold the same amount of water as other soils, without becoming water-logged. It seems likely that the mucus which a worm uses to lubricate its burrow and the passage of soil through its body, helps to cement particles together. The soil structure may also have been changed by the way that plant fibre and soil particles are mixed in the worm's gut.

Most of us will use nitrates as fertilizers but earthworms provide nitrates for the soil, too; in some cases, in fact, they may provide them in sufficient quantity for the needs of agricultural crops.

We notice earthworms mostly in our flower beds and vegetable patches but we should be particularly grateful for the work they do where we do not dig. Below fruit trees, under the lawn and in small areas of rough grass, they are busy doing the gardener's work. The few worm casts they leave on the lawn are a small price to pay for all their help.

Perhaps we should spend more time encouraging the earthworms to look after our soil. How well they do will depend upon the food that is available to them and we can always help by providing some compost. Special worm farms do breed and sell earthworms for agriculture, if you wish to increase the population of the garden quickly but, as they can multiply and spread fairly easily, most of us should not need to buy them. Occasionally, a few worms may be cut in two during digging, and we probably console ourselves by thinking that both pieces will carry on

living; but this is not necessarily true and regeneration is not successful if too many segments are amputated. Most worms cannot regenerate more than a few anterior segments although some species can have up to eighty removed from their posterior end and regenerate them.

Earthworms are killed in many ways. They are often found strewn across pavements after a heavy rain storm. Falling rain attracts them to the surface where they die, not by drowning, but because of the effects of ultra-violet radiation which penetrates their bodies. Falling rain is only one stimulus which causes them to move towards the surface; digging and walking can produce the same result, and some fishermen spread soap solution on the ground to bring them up so that they do not have to dig for their bait. Worms are also killed by other animals. They are a favourite food of moles, hedgehogs and other small mammals; thrushes, blackbirds and robins often feed on them in the garden, and other birds eat them, too. When worms come up to search for food on the surface they usually leave their tails in their burrows. When threatened, they can withdraw very quickly and then they move down into the earth, where they stay for some time. Some release foul liquids when attacked and others can cause their bodies to break in two so that one half at least can escape. Earthworms must protect themselves from severe weather. Hot, dry months are a greater problem than those which are cold and damp—it is mainly during the summer that worms move to deeper parts of the soil. Here they evacuate their guts and, after rolling up into a ball, they begin a period of inactivity which lasts until more favourable weather comes along. This is how they are sometimes found, with their bodies tied up in knots, and protected, inside a chamber lined with mucus.

Most worms are hermaphrodite, but although they are both male and female, they still usually mate with another worm rather than fertilizing themselves. They have the advantage that any member of their species they come across will be of the right sex for mating! We can tell when many species of worm are mature because they develop a prominent saddle or clitellum, about thirty segments back from the prostomium. Mating worms are attracted to each other by special scents, and they lie together on the surface with their bodies pointing in opposite directions and their anterior regions pressed together. They may stay like this for well over an hour, and, while some special long setae hold them together, others are used for mutual stimulation. Fertilization does not take place immediately but the sperm is exchanged and stored. After the worms part, they each secrete a tube around their saddles. When the tube has hardened and eggs have been deposited in it, the worm moves backwards so that the tube passes forwards along its body and is shed over its head. As the tube moves along, the eggs are fertilized by some of the stored sperm and the two ends of the tube contract to form a lemon-shaped cocoon containing the eggs. The worm goes on producing cocoons until all the stored sperm has been used up, and it will leave between five and one hundred cocoons in the upper layers of the soil each year. In dry weather they may be found in deeper soil, too. The cocoons are less

The pot worm (left) is a small, almost white worm extremely common in soil. Unlike the larger earthworms it is unable to burrow, but squeezes through cracks between the lumps of damp soil. Not all earthworms actually live in the soil: the brandling is the rather small, dark red worm found in compost heaps and other mounds of rotting and fermenting vegetation. It is readily identifiable from its smell, as it exudes an acrid yellow secretion when disturbed. The large milky worm (right) is usually found under stones or beneath the roots of mosses.

susceptible to extreme conditions than adult worms and they provide a way of preventing a population being wiped out by a long spell of severe weather. The times taken to hatch out and for the young to mature both depend upon the conditions: eggs may hatch after three weeks or take many months, and worms may mature in anything from three months to more than a year. Although worms have lived in captivity for more than ten years, their life-span in the wild is very much shorter.

Sometimes worms can be found in greater number in the region where they hatched out, but many other factors influence their distribution: there is often a concentration of them around the roots of certain plants or in a pocket of compost.

Because all earthworms are so similar in appearance and behaviour there are very few common names for them. Seen under a microscope, their differences become obvious, but some can be recognized fairly accurately with the naked eye. When there are casts on the lawn, they have almost certainly been produced by the long worm, or one of its relatives, a fairly slender creature with a flattened tail. It is usually grey-brown but its first few segments can be darker. A similar, larger, worm, which is usually more pink in colour, is the common garden worm. Others with rather distinctive colours are the blue worm, *Octrolasion cyaneum*, which has an orange clitellum and a pink tinge to its leading segments, and the milky worm, *Octrolasion lacteum*. Two smaller species are more likely to be found in rich organic soil, or in the compost heap. The brandling, *Eisenia foetida*, has deep red-brown bands alternating with lighter yellow bands and an orange clitellum. This species also releases a foul-smelling secretion when disturbed. The cockspur worm, *Dendrobaena mammalis*, is flatter in shape and has a red-violet colour which is slightly iridescent. It usually has a pale clitellum.

ALTHOUGH A SNAIL'S shell provides it with protection, it does have the disadvantage of being both cumbersome and requiring a good supply of calcium to ensure proper growth. Perhaps it is not surprising, then, that several groups of them have evolved in which the shells have become reduced so that they are now merely small particles or plates embedded in their outside coats. These animals we call slugs. Like many land invertebrates, slugs and snails must keep their bodies moist and so they are usually seen in sheltered, damp places, although they do come out into the open after a rain storm. They also come out to feed at night. Because of their shape, they are called Gastropod or 'stomach feet' molluscs. The 'foot' is the surface which makes contact with the ground, and they move by using a series of muscular contractions to glide over a mucus path which they lay for themselves. We can see where a snail has been by its glistening slime-trail. Some animals which eat snails also track them down by following their trails. The underside of the foot often looks a different colour from the rest of the animal, which can be useful for identifying the different species. Most slugs and snails have two pairs of tentacles on their heads: the smaller ones in front carry receptors which enable their owners to locate their food by its smell; the larger pair at the back carry simple eyes. Slugs move their heads from side to side and use their tentacles to find their way. Then, if they touch something unpleasant, or if they are disturbed, the tentacles are withdrawn into their heads. Being hollow, they can be pulled back like the fingers of a glove from which a hand has been hurriedly removed.

Although slugs and snails are renowned for moving slowly, they do not take their time about eating. The mouth of a snail lies beneath its head, and can be most easily seen in action on water snails when they are feeding on the algae growing on the glass side of a fish tank. As the mouth opens and closes a tooth-laden, tongue-like organ is used to scrape the food against the hard, ridged top of the snail's mouth, the radula, which works like a flexible rasp. As its teeth are worn down, a new section grows forwards, a system of tooth replacement which is not unlike that of a shark. The shape and number of teeth depend upon diet but some species have more than 20,000 on their radulae at one time.

Much of a snail's body is always kept inside its shell, called the visceral hump. When threatened, it can pull its head and foot into the shell, too. The shell resembles a spiral staircase that gets wider and wider towards the opening; just as a column runs through the centre of a spiral staircase, so the columella runs through a snail's shell. The muscle which draws the snail back into its shell is attached to the columella, which means that it cannot leave its shell but also that it is difficult for another animal to pull it out. One of the marvels of the shell is the way that it grows with the animal and provides continuous protection. Many animals with a hard outside covering have to moult as they grow, and, as a result, there are several periods during their lives when they are very vulnerable. Snails grow at different rates throughout the year and so there are a series of growth lines on their shells. When the animal is fully grown a thick lip develops around the edge and this extends to cover the centre of the spirals, which is known as the umbilicus. Nearly all shells spiral in the same way. If they are held upright so that you are looking at the opening, it will be on your right-hand side. The colour and banding may vary even in the same species. Depending upon where they live, they will need colours which absorb or reflect the sun's heat; or which will camouflage them from likely predators.

In very dry weather snails will find a hiding place and then retreat inside their shells. They cement up their openings after them which helps them to avoid drying up. Slugs cannot use this method to retain water but they have the advantage of being able to live in areas where there is too little calcium for snails to survive.

Like the earthworms, nearly all British slugs and snails are hermaphrodite. In most cases, however, they are not male and female

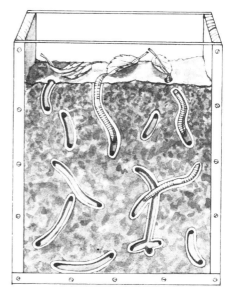

A vivarium is a dry equivalent of an aquarium for keeping land animals. This simple vivarium is used for studying earthworms. It is made by screwing or gluing two sheets of clear rigid plastic or glass to a wooden frame. There should be a space of 2–3 centimetres between the sheets, which is filled with soil. The vivarium must be covered with a thick cloth to protect the worms.

The action of the worms on the soil can be watched by adding layers of pale sand or dark peat to the soil. As the worms burrow, eating the soil and passing it out through the body, the layers become mixed, and pebbles scattered on the surface slowly sink as earth builds up around them. Sometimes the pebbles will be drawn into a pile around the mouth of a worm burrow, and this is the fate of leaves which are dragged down to be eaten at leisure.

The garlic glass snail (top two snails) lives in garden walls, rockeries and banks, as does the common or garden snail (bottom right). During the winter, these snails cluster in dry cavities to hibernate, sealing themselves into their shells with a thick mucous membrane which dries hard. In the summer they glide forth by night or after rain, on feeding forays in search of succulent leaves or fruits. The strawberry snail (centre) lives in damper situations, particularly under hedges and in strawberry beds where it can be a pest, as can the garden slug (bottom left) which also fancies other garden crops such as lettuces and tubers. This slug breeds throughout the year, laying its eggs, which look like shiny white balls, just below the surface of the soil.

at the same time and so they must pair to mate. When snails are courting they caress each other and, after a while, their tentacles droop. In many species a mating pair then fire a love dart deep into each other's bodies, like do-it-yourself cupids. The dart is usually about 12 millimetres ($\frac{1}{2}$ inch) long, made of calcium carbonate and well suited to its task by being finely ridged and tipped with a sharp point. Far from discouraging friendship, this device seems to act as a stimulus to mating. The pair approach each other and start to copulate, each inserting its penis into the other's body. Copulation may last for some hours before the animals go their separate ways. The eggs are not usually produced immediately: for instance, the garden snail mates in May or June but does not lay its eggs until July or August. The eggs are rather like miniature birds' eggs with calcium shells, and up to a hundred are laid at a time. They can be found near the surface, among plant roots or in special hollows excavated by the parents. The young hatch out from two weeks to a month later and look like tiny adults.

DESPITE THEIR REPUTATION, very few snails are guilty of damaging garden plants. One of the culprits is the common garden snail, Helix aspersa. It feeds mainly on rotting leaves but also eats fruit and vegetables which hang close to the ground. It is related to the Roman snail which appears on the menu as escargots. This dish has become so popular that there is now a market in empty shells, and doubtless, these are often filled with the flesh of other snail species and then resold to restaurants as the genuine Roman articles. We might do better to try the garden snail, which is still eaten in some parts of Britain, particularly in the Bristol area.

The other common snail which is something of a problem is the strawberry snail, Trichia striolata. This is usually about 12 millimetres ($\frac{1}{2}$ inch) high with a plain brown shell which may be quite light in colour, especially around the opening. When the snail is young the shell may be 'hairy'. Glass snails, the Oxychilus species with their glossy thin amber shells are to be found in gardens, too. They gain added protection by producing nasty smelling secretions—which is how the garlic glass snail got its name! Glass snails feed on a range of foods which includes fungi as well as rotting animal flesh.

The idea of eating snails may not appeal to many people but some scientists think that they could become an important source of food for humans and animals in the future: they would certainly be a more efficient source of food than the livestock we keep at present, although some sales resistance might be expected. Snails are proving to be useful to man in other ways, in the meantime: they are the source of a large number of substances used in medicine, and they have a place in various fields of research, particularly in genetics.

Slugs probably have the worst reputation of all garden animals but, once again, there are only about three species which have earned the group its bad name. These are the netted slug, Agriolimax reticulatus;

the garden slug, *Arion hortensis* and the Budapest slug,
Milox budapestensis. The first two species are fairly small but the
Budapest slug may be 5 centimetres (2 inches) long. The really
large slugs which we often find in our gardens are the large black
slug, the large red slug and the great grey slug—the last may be
up to 20 centimetres (8 inches) long, which is only half the size
of the largest British slug, the ash-black *Limax cinerao niger*.
These large slugs cannot be considered pests as they feed
mainly on fungi and dead leaves.

The great grey slug, the netted slug and the Budapest slug
have a keel running from their tails for at least some way
along their backs. They all evolved from a different group of
snails than the round-backed slugs already mentioned. A third
group have the remnant of a shell on their tail. They are
carnivorous and can alter their shape quickly, which helps

Arion ater *is a very large slug which can vary in colour from completely black to grey, orange or brick-red. Black specimens seem to be commonest in the north, red specimens more common in the south. This slug lives in all sorts of different habitats from grassland and moors to hedges and woods, and is also commonly found in gardens. When irritated it contracts into a spherical blob less than half its extended length, and may rock from side to side for a considerable time.*

them to follow their prey through the soil and also to swallow their food more easily. These carnivores, the *Testacella* species, feed mainly on earthworms.

Some species of slugs have a rather spectacular way of mating. For example, the great grey slug and some of its relatives wrap themselves in a mucus sheet which they can use to suspend their bodies in the air. They can mate while lowering themselves to the ground as they perform a 'love dance'. Slugs that have lost their love dart may still have a special stimulating device which they can extend during courtship.

A large slug with white mites swarming all over it may seem to be getting its just reward. The mites even go in and out of the respiratory opening but they do not seem to do the animal any harm. It cannot be denied that some slugs are pests but they may do some good as well for as they burrow, sometimes fairly deeply, they may help to incorporate organic material in the soil. They also produce large quantities of mucus and this probably helps the soil structure. Remember that even harmful species often prefer to eat mainly decaying vegetation so, in general, they do not really deserve their bad reputation.

The Hidden World

During the spring and autumn, almost any work in the garden will uncover a host of animals. Not that they remain visible for long, for after a few moments of hopping, scattering and slithering in all directions, most of them will have disappeared. This range of escape methods provides a glimpse of the animals' varying ways of life, and reminds us of the activity which is going on continuously below ground. Although the kinds of animals we uncover will depend upon where we are busy—whether we are moving pots, digging or working on the compost heap—they will nearly all belong to the same group, the *Arthropods*.

The *Arthropods* are the largest phylum (major grouping in the animal kingdom) of all, and were among the first to leave the sea when life evolved. Their characteristic jointed legs and hard exoskeletons (hard outer covering), which had been so useful in the sea, gave them the means to walk about on land and yet not dry up too quickly. Now, after hundreds of millions of years, some of them—insects, spiders and scorpions—are able to survive out in the open dry air for long periods of time, while the rest must spend most of their lives in humid places. During the day this usually means taking cover, but at night, when the air is moist, some of them may come up to the surface. Many will keep moving unless they feel that their bodies are completely surrounded by solid material, which is usually soil. For them darkness provides the same reassurance as light does for us. These, then, are the hidden animals. Unfortunately, they have been introduced to nearly all of us at a young age as the creepy-crawlies, furtive, skulking creatures of the dark. An unfair reputation, for we know that many of them are our helpers in the garden, and very few have been shown to do much real damage.

One of the most common and easily recognizable of the hidden garden animals is the wood-louse. Wood-lice are plentiful in the compost heap and under any brick or piece of wood which has remained on the ground for more than a few days. They are frequent visitors to sheds, garages and houses and they can be seen climbing walls and plants, particularly during summer evenings. Of course, they are not actually lice or even insects but relatives of shrimps and crabs. As such, they are among the few crustaceans to live on dry land, and therefore hold a special fascination for zoologists. Wood-lice also do a great deal of work for the gardener. They feed up on plant

At night or under very humid conditions by day, small invertebrates trundle forth to feed. Centipedes (left and right) hunt smaller animals, which they grasp with powerful poison claws. The cylindrical slow-moving millipede (centre) is an inoffensive muncher of rotting plant material, as is the largest British woodlouse Oniscus asellus *(several are on log, left). The common earwig (on log, right) is omnivorous: when seen in flowerheads or fruit it may be pursuing insects. The shiny pill-millipede (bottom centre) can roll up into a tight impregnable ball when attacked, as can the pill-bug or pill-woodlouse (bottom right).*

material which has already started to decay and so help in the breakdown process which replenishes the soil with the foods needed by growing plants: their feeding habits can get them a bad reputation because they are sometimes caught clearing up the remains of cuttings and bulbs which have been killed in other ways. It is, however, very rare for wood-lice to eat any living plant material, and when they are found climbing fruit bushes or wandering in the flower beds, they are usually looking for suitable places to shelter.

All wood-lice have seven pairs of legs and almost elliptical, flat shapes. In any group there will be variations in colour and texture, for these animals change as they mature and sometimes more than one species can be found living together. As adults most of them are grey or grey-brown in appearance, but whites, oranges and reds can all be found. There are over forty species in Britain but, of these, two are most common and widespread, and another group is worth mentioning because it is so easy to recognize. *Porcellio scaber* is a common species which prefers dry habitats; *Oniscus asellus* is more likely to be found in damper surroundings. The latter is often grey and has rough

spots covering its body but it also has many other colours. (Wood-lice often show their greatest divergence from the common colour in gardens near the sea.) The group which can be easily recognized is the pill bugs, which can curl up into a tight ball when disturbed. The most common of them is *Armadillidium*, a name that reminds us of the armadillo which also protects itself in this way.

Wood-lice must moult as they grow and their translucent discarded exoskeletons are sometimes found close by their owners although they are also quite often eaten by them. Moulting is a complicated business but an animal in the process of shedding can be easily recognized: it will have different coloured halves because the rear half is shed first and for a time the back area has the animal's typical colour, while the front has a milky appearance.

Porcellio scaber *is one of the large and very common wood-lice found under loose bark, in rockeries, even in the cellars of houses, or, as here, under damp sacking in a garden shed. It even lives quite commonly on sand dunes. Like all wood-lice, its cuticle is not waterproof so it congregates anywhere damp enough for its wellbeing. Normally it is active by night, but if its daytime home should start to dry out it will emerge to hunt for a damper, safer retreat. Wood-lice grow slowly, with periodic moults, and are not fully grown until about two years old. When the cuticle is about to be shed it appears white after lifting away from the new, darker cuticle beneath, so that a wood-louse in mid-moult appears piebald.*

Although the behaviour of the wood-louse is quite complicated, a fairly simple set of patterns serves to keep it in a suitable environment. If it is in a light, dry place it tends to walk quickly and in straight lines. In more hospitable surroundings its behaviour is just the opposite: it turns often and moves only slowly. On balance, this keeps the animal where it is content and makes it likely to leave a threatening area.

When they are uncovered or attacked, wood-lice have several ways of defending themselves. Some have quite long legs and can run away from danger; others will clamp down and are difficult, even impossible, for some animals to pick up. Its whole shape gives it stability and makes it difficult to turn or to hold on to. *Armadillidium* and the other pill bugs have already been mentioned: once they have curled up they are safe from many predators although not from those that can open their mouths wide enough to take the 'pill' all in one go. Some other types of wood-lice might actually reach the mouth of a predator, only to be released again because they have produced some fairly foul substances which make them distasteful. One species which lives in ants' nests probably uses this method to ensure that it is not troubled. It is well known that possums feign death when threatened, and wood-lice, too, are believed to 'play possum'. A strange expression in a way, as most of us have never even seen a possum and yet must have seen wood-lice or millipedes feigning death.

Most of the behaviour of the wood-louse will not be witnessed by the gardener as it only takes place under cover. Mating, for instance, lasts only a few minutes. A short affair. The male courts the female by 'patting' and 'nibbling' her and then mounts her, first from one side then the other. The young develop in the female's brood pouch and leave her body as miniature adults. They mature after a series of moults and may live for several years although, in the wild, eighteen months is considered exceptional.

CENTIPEDES CAN ALSO be found in the garden or in outbuildings at most times of the year. They bear a superficial resemblance to millipedes (all those legs!) but otherwise they are really quite different animals. Compared to the millipede's cylindrical body, the centipede's is quite flat. We associate the animals together mainly because they both have so many legs but even here there are differences for the millipedes have two pairs of legs on most of their segments and the centipedes have only one. A close look at the front of the centipede shows us two pincers attached to the segment behind the head. These extend forward, bulging out at the sides so that from above they give the animal the appearance of having huge cheeks. These 'poison claws' are found on all centipedes, most of which are voracious carnivores. The millipedes, on the other hand, are herbivorous and do not have claws.

In their diet the centipedes will include a variety of potential pests, so they are welcomed by the knowledgeable gardener. They do not all

hunt in the same way, but use methods at least as diverse as those used by the predatory mammals. For instance, the group that is uncovered most often under stones on the surface, and which I find in the coalbunker during the winter, contains the stone-living forms or *Lithobiomorphs*. To many people, these are probably the typical centipedes. They are built for speed, which they use to escape their enemies and to catch their food. Often there is no more than a few seconds in which to watch them before they disappear, and if we try to delay them, we find that their slender shape makes them quite difficult to hold on to. Although there are seventeen species of stone-living centipedes in Britain, they are all very similar, with the same attractive red-brown colour as a horse-chestnut which has just been released from its spiny husk. Their bodies are relatively short and inflexible with fifteen pairs of fairly long legs which increase in length towards the tail, an arrangement which lessens the chance of them tripping themselves up. *Lithobiomorphs* hunt for their food, which includes slugs, insect larvae, mites and worms, using touch and smell more than sight. They also eat other centipedes. Although they have eyes, they cannot see well and their legs, especially the back pair, as well as their long antennae, are extremely sensitive.

Members of the largest group of British centipedes are more likely to be discovered while a gardener is digging, because they live in the

Many insects and other small animals are active at night, although they are often seen fleeing to safety while you garden. Their presence in the garden can be discovered by sinking pitfall traps in the ground. A steep-sided plastic flowerpot or yoghurt container is suitable. Some animals will just fall into the trap as they wander about but they can be attracted by using an apple core or a dead animal as bait.

A dor beetle is about to fall in and join a centipede and an earwing.

soil. They are called *Geophilomorphs* or soil-loving forms. They cannot be mistaken for their relatives on the surface since they have much longer, narrow bodies and far more pairs of legs—there are always more than thirty-seven and there can be as many as one hundred and one pairs. They vary in colour from a bright straw to dark brown but their heads are nearly always dark. The leading section of the body is narrower with thicker legs than the rear two-thirds. All the legs are short when compared to those of the *Lithobiomorphs* and the animals are therefore sluggish in their movements, but there are few places below ground where an animal of this size could use long legs to move quickly anyway. It weaves its way between the soil particles. Having located a crevice with its antennae or sensitive back legs, it enters the tunnel and expands its body to widen its path. To help them, *Geophilomorphs* have extremely flexible bodies which can loop many times along their length. The short antennae are continuously active as the animal moves. If its forward path is blocked, the animal searches with its back legs and, should it discover a way to the rear, it moves backwards. It seems to be able to go in this way just as well as it can forwards. Being without even the simple eyes of the *Lithobiomorphs*, the soil-loving forms find their way entirely by touch and smell.

THE *SCOLOPENDROMORPHS* FORM the remaining group of centipedes. They are light brown and have twenty-one pairs of legs. Although they are in many ways intermediate between the *Geophilomorphs* and the *Lithobiomorphs*, they are probably more like the latter. The British species, like all our own centipedes, are quite harmless but tropical varieties can inflict nasty wounds which have, in a very few cases, been fatal.

When any of the centipedes come across suitable prey they grasp it between their poison claws. Sometimes, especially with larger animals such as slugs and worms, there may be quite a struggle. Once this is over, the centipede can use its poison claws together with special mouthparts for holding and manipulating the food while pieces are 'bitten' off by its mandibles.

Centipedes do not have a courtship as we would know it. In fact, most mating pairs do not even meet each other. The male produces a bag of sperm, called a spermatophore, and deposits it in a web. The female may be attracted to the web by smell. She has special legs on her terminal segments for catching up the spermatophore. The *Lithobiomorphs* do not stay with the eggs once they have been laid. They lay them individually and cover them with mucus and soil which they have crushed in their special terminal legs. This gives the eggs excellent camouflage and, when the young hatch out, they are fairly advanced miniature adults with stubby legs and poison claws. The other centipedes enlarge hollows in the ground or a piece of wood to make a nest. The mother lays her eggs and then provides protection by coiling her body round them. She will clean the eggs from time to time, and this activity seems to be very important because any eggs which are left uncleaned are soon attacked by fungus. Even when the young have hatched out the mother remains with them for a time. During the whole of this nesting period, which can last for well over a month, she does not leave the nest even to look for food. However, if disturbed, a mother centipede's behaviour can quickly change and she may eat the eggs. This 'denning up' and stopping feeding is reminiscent of some higher animals such as the polar bear. During the early summer, we are quite likely to come across the nest of a centipede in the garden. The young are left when they can fend for themselves and although their appearance never changes drastically thoughout their lives, they go through a series of moults before they mature, after about three years. The animals might then live for a further year or two.

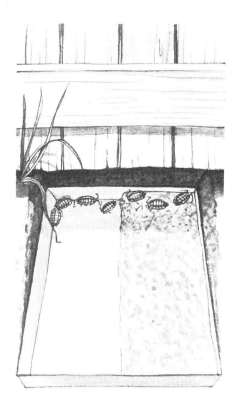

THE MOST COMMON of the British millipedes are the shiny black ones which have long cylindrical bodies and curl up when they are disturbed. Once they feel secure they unwind and move off slowly on their short, light-coloured legs. There are many species which this description fits and, as a group, they are called the *Iuliform* millipedes. Despite their wide distribution, there are times when they seem almost to have disappeared from the garden and yet we can still find other millipedes with dusky brown bodies and shield-like edges to their backs. This is just another reminder of how the activities of many of the hidden animals are controlled by temperature and, more especially, humidity.

The millipedes' numerous short legs enable them to force a way through the soil, rather as a group of men can break a path for themselves with a battering ram. Special reinforced plates, beneath which the animal tucks its head, provide a sort of crash helmet. The animal's exoskeleton contains calcium which makes it much stronger than that of a centipede. At the same time it means that millipedes are more restricted to soils that are calcium-rich. Once a cylindrical millipede has bulldozed a tunnel with its head region, the rest of the body can easily follow because they are nearly always the same thickness all the way along. Like the centipedes, millipedes must avoid getting their legs tangled and this is accomplished by there being a split second between the time that neighbouring feet are lifted: the effect of this can be seen as a series of waves which pass back along the legs when the animal moves. Although almost all millipedes have a cylindrical form, some of them are given a flat appearance by keels which extend along each side of their backs. The flat-backed millipedes, as they are called, have a somewhat different way of moving from the cylindrical forms. They insert their heads into a crevice and then use their keels to split open a path for themselves, a method not dissimilar to the way we might use a wedge to split wood along its grain.

Flat-backed millipedes are usually found in rather different habitats from their more rounded relatives—in rotting wood, beneath bark,

Compared with insects, woodlice have skins which are not completely waterproof, so they come out at night when it is cool and humid. During the day they hide under stones or under bark where the atmosphere keeps very moist. The behaviour of woodlice is governed by simple rules which are easy to demonstrate. If half a dozen woodlice are put in a flat tin or dish with damp soil on one side and dry on the other, they will eventually congregate in the wet half. (Provide a sheet of glass placed on top to keep them in.) If one half is then shaded, the woodlice retreat from the light. They also like to press themselves in an angle, like the edge of the dish or against each other. In this way, the woodlice are guided into cool, dark crevices and crannies where the conditions will be most favourable.

among leaf litter, and anywhere else where there are layers that will yield to the splitting technique. Being herbivorous, millipedes do not have poison claws and their jaws are not particularly strong. It seems unlikely that they are able to bite through the hard outside layers of most healthy plants but some of them can eat seedlings and the tips of roots. They can also attack ripe fruits and tubers which have already been damaged by disease or by animals. However, mostly they eat fungus and rotting plant material preferring, in nearly all cases, to eat leaves which have remained on the ground for many months, although they will eat the remains of dead animals as well. Perhaps this is a warning against being too tidy in the garden!

Certain conditions do seem to encourage millipedes to damage plants. Often these are at their most vulnerable during the spring when the humidity and temperature of the soil is favourable to millipedes as well as to plant growth. For similar reasons, millipedes are often numerous in heavy soils and in greenhouses. Sometimes they are thought to damage plants when they are searching for moisture in dry spells. However, against the damage done by a small number of

species, we must weigh their ability to speed up the return of nutrients to the soil and count them as welcome residents, at least of the compost heap. In the future we might find other uses for them because there is some evidence that they are sensitive to certain pollutants and could provide us with an early warning system.

Most millipedes build a nest when they are about to lay their eggs. Often the site chosen is lined in some way, and many mud caves are given hardened walls with a mixture of saliva and some of the animal's own waste products. The nests can also be found under rocks, bark, logs and sometimes—to the dismay of the gardeners—in ripe fruit. Many flat-backed millipedes stay with their eggs for a short time but most other species abandon them after laying. When the young hatch out they look more like maggots than millipedes, and they pass through a series of stages before they are fully grown. These stages are separated by moults and, during each stage, several pairs of legs and several segments are added to the body. A nest, similar to the sort used for the eggs, is used by most millipedes to provide them with protection when they are moulting. The nest probably also helps to prevent them from losing too much water during a dry spell. Once a millipede's exoskeleton has dried out, it is better able to resist desiccation than is a centipede and so it can be active in drier soils.

Millipedes get together for mating and during their courtship they use scents, back-tapping and a kind of licking. These help the animals to recognize each other correctly and provide a stimulation. If the female is receptive to the male's advances she will, like many other animals, adopt a suitable posture. Should she not be in the mood, however, she does not have to put up with her suitor's attention for long. She just gives him a blast with some of her defensive repellents—the exact opposite of the way in which our own species uses a perfume spray!

Most species of millipedes and centipedes have more than one line of defence but they usually have a special method in which they excel. Often they will curl up like a watch spring when they are disturbed. For an animal with the sort of armour plating that will enable it to crash its way through the soil, this is no mean feat. They will stay in the coiled position, with their legs tightly tucked in, until the danger is past and then they will slowly uncoil. They manage this, using the same technique that enables them to spiral their bodies as they move through the soil. The pill millipede, as its name suggests, rolls up into a ball in the same way as a pill bug. It can be distinguished from the pill bug because it has more than twice as many legs, its body has a more oval shape and it is darker and more shiny in colour.

Like many of the centipedes, most millipedes can produce repellent secretions from special glands on their bodies, sometimes called 'stink-glands'. The name hardly does their powers justice: they can produce a series of substances which may smell nasty, taste revolting, irritate the skin and contain a range of poisons, including hydro cyanic acid. (Some tropical species can be dangerous, but in Britain we are let off

Geophilomorphs *are very elongated centipedes with as many as a hundred pairs of short legs. They are blind, not very active animals, usually found in damp places. Females protect their eggs in a nest and coil themselves around them, occasionally cleaning the eggs to remove bacteria and fungus spores which would otherwise kill the developing embryos.*

The spotted snake millipede has no eyes and yet is sensitive to light, for if uncovered it will continue to crawl until it finds itself in darkness again. It normally lives away from light in the soil and beneath stones. It is the commonest millipede of arable land and vegetable gardens, and can be something of a pest when it attacks root crops. Its jaws are too small to gnaw through the tough skin of, for instance, a potato, but if a hole has already been made by a wireworm or other pest, the millipede can enter. Over a hundred spotted snake millipedes have been counted in one single potato.

lightly.) Zoologists refer to the glands which produce all these 'goodies' as repugnatorial glands. Some of the animals which have this effective defence mechanism advertise their nastiness by having special colouring and in this way they are able to enjoy a quieter life, as potential predators quickly learn to recognize them and leave them alone. Just as the skunk is easily recognized by its black and white stripes, so the cylindrical spotted snake millipede is unmistakable because of the bright red spots it carries on the sides of its body. This device might work well once a millipede has been uncovered and is lit by the sun, but they spend most of their lives in the dark.

Perhaps, then, we should not be surprised that some of them can produce light-emitting substances. The secretions which emit the light are often released when the animals are disturbed at night, and at times the light is so bright that they have become known as glow-worms. Of course, the real owner of this name is a beetle. (This is not the only instance of there being confusion between millipedes and beetles: some people call millipedes wire-worms—a name that really belongs to the larvae of a click beetle.) We are only just learning about the many different species of animals that produce light and then use it in their daily lives. For example, many animals deep in the oceans use it to communicate with each other, and it is likely that some millipedes use light in a similar way. An autumn evening is the time when this phenomenon is most likely to be observed.

The wood-lice, centipedes and millipedes are all armed with such an array of defensive mechanisms that it is not surprising that they are often left alone by predatory animals. At the same time, birds, small mammals and amphibians do often feed on them. Other predators, such as spiders, seem to make a meal of them when there is nothing more tasty available.

SOME OF THE animals that we come across in the garden, particularly in the compost heap or in that shaded corner that always seems to stay on the damp side, are really too small for us to study with the naked eye. At the same time, they are very noticeable and what brings them to our attention is their activity. They also show up because they are white and so contrast with the dark colour of rich, damp soil. Most of these animals were once thought to be primitive insects. They lack wings and so cannot fly but, even so, some of them take to the air when alarmed. These are the surface-living Collembolans. Each one has a forked spring-organ on its tail which is folded under the body and locked into position when not in use. A small muscular contraction unlocks the spring-organ and the animal is propelled into the air. Collembolans that live below ground cannot spring and, since they lack burrowing equipment, they must move through the existing pores in the soil. Living among the surface Collembolans are some other small white animals which run for cover. Some of them are probably the Pauropods. Both Collembolans and Pauropods eat a range of decaying plant and animal food and fungi.

There are many other animals that spend at least part of their lives in the soil. The larvae of beetles and other insects, slugs and worms are examples of some of the animals which we are likely to come across, but which have been mentioned elsewhere in this book. We cannot pretend that all of these animals are welcome in our gardens but very few of them are serious pests. Many of them contribute to the mechanical breakdown of organic material and they may make a small contribution to humification. As they tunnel their way through the soil, they also improve its structure by breaking it down and improving aeration and drainage.

Not all animals choose the soil as a hiding place. Earwigs, for example, are often found among the petals of flowers, although they are more likely to be found underground in the winter. Perhaps it is this choice of hiding place or those long pincers on their tails which make earwigs animals which many people loathe. They do eat petals, together with many other foods, for they are true omnivores, but they hardly do sufficient damage to warrant their reputation.

Perhaps the largest group of animals that remain hidden from us for most of the time are those that use camouflage. For most of us there are still some animals in our own gardens which we have yet to discover because they are so well concealed by their shape and colour. Do we really need to be shown a film of animals from a distant continent to find interest in the wonders of nature?

The Role of the Naturalist

The preceding chapters show the varied range of wildlife which can be found within the confines of the garden. The full tally is almost as long as the lists of animals which have been recorded in the whole of the British Isles (seashore life being the main exception). The important point is that, wherever it is and whatever its state, the garden has plenty of interest for anyone to find. The animals are literally on your doorstep so there is no need to mount expeditions into the countryside to undertake the study of wildlife. In this chapter, some suggestions will be given of what can be looked for and studied in the garden.

In using your garden for studying wildlife you will be following in the footsteps of pioneers of natural history. Jean Henri Fabre, for instance, who died in 1915 at Serignan in France, has left charming accounts of the animals he studied. He delved into the private lives of insects, discovering how they lived, and he tells his readers how he made his observations. This is important. When I was first becoming interested in natural history, I would be fascinated by somebody's account of an animal's life and habits but it would leave me frustrated. How, I wanted to know, should I set about seeing the same things for myself? The text would be silent. Nowadays, the budding naturalist is not left unaided; there are plenty of books and magazine articles designed to cater for those with a desire to do something practical.

Learning by observation and experiment leads to a fuller understanding of a subject and, once something has been seen in the flesh, it is instantly more memorable than if it was culled only from the pages of a book. Then, when the observation has been made, confirming what was described in the book, further enquiries may reveal new facts not given there and the thrill of discovery is achieved. It is difficult to find a match for the excitement of discovering something for yourself and of experiencing the satisfaction and achievement that Archimedes must have felt when he leaped from his bath shouting 'Eureka'! It may later transpire that someone else has already made the discovery; it may even be common knowledge, but the thrill of personal discovery is still there.

The garden naturalist is very well placed to make truly original discoveries. There are large gaps in our knowledge of the smaller inhabitants—the insects and other invertebrate animals. Their exact distribution over the British Isles is not always well known, and details of the habits of many are often a mystery. Fabre showed how these can be unravelled with little more than patient observation and his methods are still adequate for the garden researcher. Among the 'higher animals', there is less scope, although the pages of ornithological journals show that the study of garden birds is still rewarding.

The garden is a particularly fruitful place for original observation of unusual quirks in animal behaviour. Regular habits, such as feeding or courting, are easy to study. The behaviour of garden birds, for instance, is described in many books and is there for all to see. Yet animals sometimes behave peculiarly and, because there is no regularity in unusual behaviour, it is difficult to study systematically. The solution is to collect scattered eyewitness accounts and look for a pattern.

One puzzle sometimes found in gardens is small piles of pebbles which prove to be neatly arranged to form a tiny cairn over the entrance to a mousehole or inside the burrow. It is built by the common wood mouse or long-tailed fieldmouse and some of the pebbles weigh as much as the mouse. If the cairn is dismantled and its pebbles scattered, the mouse rebuilds it. The crux of the puzzle is that cairns are built only on rare occasions. If they had some obvious function, such as protection from predators or heavy rain, we should expect to find them over most holes. A possibility is that the mice may build them to keep other mice from raiding their hoards of seeds, but this can be confirmed only by investigating many instances of cairn-building.

Another strange quirk of behaviour which is encountered mainly in the garden is the peculiar habit among birds of tapping on windows with their beaks. Sometimes the shiny hubcap of a car, or the driving mirror, is substituted for the window. Such attacks are witnessed in hundreds of gardens each year. The standard explanation is that a cock bird mistakes its reflection for a rival intruding on its territory. This may be correct in many instances but it is not the complete answer, for hen birds also peck at windows. Then there are the strange cases of carrion crows which persistently attack one particular window with such violence that the pane is splattered with blood and mucus.

T HE THRILL OF discovery is by no means essential to the enjoyment of natural history. The animals and plants can be enjoyed merely for their own sakes but the enjoyment is increased if we have some idea of what we are looking at. A little planning is necessary, so that we know what to look for and have some background information to assist in understanding what we find. These are generalizations which apply to all natural history studies but the garden has a particular appeal because you do not have to travel.

Nothing could be simpler. Get up, go outside and start peering about. Lift up a log and see what is living there (probably wood-lice, earwigs and centipedes but, with luck, a mouse or vole in a nest of

The behaviour of ants and aphids can be watched in comfort by cutting off a stem and bringing it indoors to examine it under a magnifying glass. The aphids will be seen with their needle-like mouthparts inserted into the stem. They suck the plant's sap and the excess fluid is excreted from the rear of the aphids as drops of sweet honeydew. A bright light reveals the drops being flicked off as tiny points of brilliance which speed off in a high arc. The ants visit the aphids to drink the honeydew and carry it back to the nest.

133

Conspicuous in the long grass are the frog-hoppers, little insects frog-like in appearance and in jumping ability (top). They are the well-known 'cuckoo-spit insects', whose larvae secrete a frothy mass of puddles around themselves (on grass blade beside snail). Several species of harvestman (among grasses) may live here, some with quite excessively long legs. They hunt by night

grass). Look closely at some flowers, and find out which insects are visiting them to sip the nectar. A pocket magnifying glass with × 8 magnification will reveal plenty of detail but you have to get very near the object, which may take flight. A lower power lens, of the sort used by philatelists, is quite adequate for watching insects and has the advantage that it has a large field of view and you can keep your distance. Combine these investigations with gardening. Watch carefully while digging and weeding, because many animals will be disturbed and sent scurrying for cover. The pupae of moths, grubs of beetles, snails' eggs and tight knots of resting worms will come to light as you turn the soil. Alternatively, if this is too strenuous, settle into a garden seat and keep watch. It can be very instructive. Konrad Lorenz describes sitting in front of an aquarium and staring into it as into the flames of a fire: 'All conscious thought is happily lost in this state of apparent vacancy, and yet, in these hours of idleness, one learns essential truths about the macrocosm and the microcosm.'

The same holds true for sitting in gardens, and the key phrase is 'apparent vacancy'. The idleness is physical, not mental, as the senses must remain alert and the mind questioning. Having found some interesting-looking animal, or plant, ask what it is doing, or what it might do, and why. Such questions are easier to ask if one has some idea of what to look for. Go back indoors or retire to a seat with suitable books. The best are those which give plenty of information about the habits of a rather limited number of animals. From these books we learn that the earwig under the log broods its babies, or that short, open flowers, such as speedwell, attract hoverflies whose tiny mouthparts cannot deal with long, tubular flowers, and that the flies' stripes of yellow and black are designed to fool birds into thinking that they have the dangerous attributes of a wasp.

It is quite a thrill to find an animal doing something and to know the explanation of what it is doing and why. (Astound your family and friends as well!) In other words, confirm for yourself what you have read or been told. It is good to know that a tiny, delicate snail often dug out of compost heaps can be identified by its strong smell of garlic. Not unexpectedly, it is called the garlic glass snail. And armed with some background reading on ants, you can seek out a rose or other plants where aphids are feeding on sap. Hold the stem steady, watch the ants and aphids and you will see one of the wonders of the garden.

While examining aphids' colonies there is a chance of seeing the attacks of predators, such as lacewings, hoverfly larvae and ladybirds, the last-named in both the familiar spotted adult form and as larvae, slug-like and pleated concertina-fashion. Even better, close scrutiny may show the aphids reproduc-ing—a fascinating sight. Reproduction is a very rapid process so it is not too difficult, with a little patience and perseverance, to find an aphid in the process of giving birth. The baby appears to bud from the rear end of the mother but is actually being extruded, like spaghetti. Gradually its legs and antennae unfurl and it drops off to join its elder siblings feeding in a cluster around the mother.

and rest by day. Under stones and bark can be found a variety of wood-lice and centipedes, staying in the damp by day and coming out to forage at night. Also nocturnal is the wood mouse or long-tailed field mouse (bottom right) whose nest of shredded grasses is snuggly tucked beneath a piece of rotton wood.

Pottering around the garden without any plan in mind can be rewarding but it is easy to miss things. This is where a little preparation is very profitable. If you can be sufficiently well-organized, browse through some natural history books early in the year, and plan what to look for and when, so avoiding disappointment later. It is annoying, when a row of poplars inspires a fancy to look for poplar hawk-moths, to find that the adults were on the wing two months earlier. Therefore, a list of what may be found at various seasons, having regard to the environment of your garden, should be kept where it will not be forgotten. My preparations for the year always include listening to records of birdsong and, later, thumbing through flower books to remind myself of what I have forgotten during the winter.

HAVE A REGARD also for the best conditions under which to look for particular animals. The heat of the day is a tempting time to go into the garden but many animals prefer to keep cool and remain inactive at this time. Birds feed and sing mainly in the early morning and evening. Butterflies are an obvious exception to this generalization, but moths are best seen in the evening when, in the words of the writer, W. H. Hudson, they go about their flowery business, and bats come out to hunt them. One summer evening there was a fly-past of noctules. It was repeated on successive evenings at approximately the same time and always coming from the same direction, so I took to stationing myself farther back along their route each day until I saw them tumbling out of their roost in an old woodpecker's hole.

The hours of darkness bring out the slimy animals. A dim light and a soft tread are needed to catch them unawares. Earthworms ease out of their burrows on warm, damp nights in search of food and mates, but their rear ends are firmly anchored and they can retract in a twinkling. Fallen leaves are grasped in the mouth and pulled back into the burrow, where they can be seen in the morning sticking up like marker flags. Mating is accomplished in a sticky embrace in which each of the partners fertilizes the other and both later lay eggs. The worms may be attacked by carnivorous slugs, while slime trails show where other slugs have climbed trees in search of edible fungi.

If the study of garden natural history requires preparation, it also deserves recording. It may seem rather pointless to make records, which might never be re-read, of casual observations, which might never be repeated, but there are sound reasons to keep a 'nature diary', however brief and scattered are its entries. It is often useful to be able to refer back to previous years and check when butterflies and flowers appeared, birds started singing and so on. The recording of an event also ensures that it is properly observed in respect to time, numbers, what happened and, above all, identification. The enjoyment and value of observations are hugely improved if there is a commitment to

Aphids are tiny bugs that feed by sucking sap. A by-product of their feeding is a sweet secretion called honeydew. Many sorts of ants seek out and collect this honeydew where the aphids have scattered it, but other ant species known as pastoral ants actually milk the aphids for it. An ant will caress a gorged aphid with its antennae, whereupon the aphid voids a droplet of honeydew which the ant consumes. An aphid that is repeatedly milked produces more honeydew than an untended aphid. In return for this sweet food, the ants protect the aphids, driving off would-be predators by spraying with formic acid, or even picking up the aphids and carrying them to safety.

136

find out the names of species seen. It is all too easy to see a butterfly, for example, watch it flutter past, enjoy its beauty and leave it at that—without any idea what kind of butterfly it was.

A commitment to check identification can be ensured by a programme of systematic recording. Butterflies lend themselves well to this scheme. A daily record of butterflies seen throughout the year will show the pattern of emergence times and, if the record is to be made complete, every single butterfly must be chased and identified. The first to appear are the small tortoiseshells, brimstones and peacocks which hibernate as adults. (Incidentally, the naming of

Because it hibernates as an adult, the brimstone is one of the first butterflies to appear in the spring and one of the last to be seen on the wing in autumn. It hibernates among evergreen leaves, well camouflaged by its leaf-like outline and coloration. The sulphur-yellow males emerge first, followed later by the paler, greenish-white females. Although the butterflies are frequently seen feeding at garden flowers such as hyacinths, this is typically a woodland species. The eggs are laid singly on buckthorn. The green caterpillars are inconspicuous as they rest along the midrib of the leaves, and the pupae, which are green and extremely leaf-like, are also excellently camouflaged.

insects and plants is an interesting sideline. These butterflies are named for their colourings. Brimstone is an old word for sulphur, which is yellow, and the brimstone's colour gave this whole butterfly tribe its name.) Other species appear as they emerge from chrysalises or immigrate from continental Europe, and some species produce two generations of adults in a year, even a third in the best summers. Over the years, charts of butterfly flying times show the effects of bad spells of weather and the records can be expanded to include the flowers which the butterflies visit. They have their preferences but will there also be a sequence as flowers bloom and wither? As I write, in early September, the tortoiseshells and peacocks in my garden are deserting the fading buddleias for newly opened ice plants.

From making the observations systematic, as with the butterflies, it is only a short step to starting special projects and experiments. They can be short-term and involving perhaps an hour or so, or long-term and continuing for years if necessary. There are many books which give suggestions for projects on wildlife. They may not be aimed specifically at the garden naturalist but some projects either fit the garden situation or can be adapted. The garden can also be used as a proving-ground for projects which can then be taken into the countryside. The following suggestions of things to do have been chosen mainly because they are simple, do not require sophisticated equipment or expertise, and can be done in most gardens.

THE PLANT KINGDOM is the neglected half of the living world. Despite the abundance and variety of plants, coupled with the fact that the animal kingdom would collapse without them, there are remarkably few books about them when compared with the vast array on animals. The exception is books on horticulture. The reason for the lack of books on plants is easy to see. Plants do not do much, they just grow, blossom and set seed. Texts on plants, therefore, tend to do little more than describe them and discuss the ecological conditions in which they grow. This is a pity, because plants do some interesting things; it is unfortunate that none of our three native insect-eating plants are likely to be found in gardens and we have to settle for more prosaic species.

Perhaps the obvious project, and certainly the most suitable for a garden, is to grow plants. Growing oaks from acorns or sycamores from keys (dry, winged fruits) is interesting in its own right, but growing particular plants has the added advantage that they serve to attract animals by providing home or food—stinging nettles for caterpillars of various butterflies, for instance. The two most interesting parts of a plant's life are the pollination of its flowers and the dispersion of its seeds. Flowering plants and insects evolved together to produce elaborate mechanisms for their mutual advantage: the insects get nectar and pollen to eat and the plants get their pollen transferred from flower to flower for cross-fertilization. The colour and

arrangement of the petals,
which are so pleasing to our
eyes, and the delicate odours,
are designed to attract insects.
In some plants the pollination
mechanism is simple, as in the ice
plant and Michaelmas daisy, which
become covered with tiny flies and
beetles as well as bumblebees and
butterflies. Others have a flower that
is discriminating; only heavy bumblebees can force their way into a snap-
dragon, and cuckoo-pints (or lords and
ladies) imprison flies until they have done
their job. The investigation of these
mechanisms requires recourse to a plant
book, followed by sallies into the garden, and
the same is true for the study of seed dispersal.

Fruits, berries, nuts, pips, stones and seeds are
common words but without basic botanical knowledge it is not easy to appreciate the difference. The
seed is the part which grows into the new plant and a
fruit is the part which encloses it. A berry is a kind of fruit
and a nut is a dry fruit, as compared with the fleshy fruit of
a plum. The situation is confused by the scientific inaccuracy of
common English: blackberries are not true berries (like bilber-
ries) and walnuts are not true nuts (like hazelnuts). However, the
essential point is that the covering of the seed helps in its dispersal and
the garden provides many examples. Hazelnuts and acorns can disperse
themselves only as far as they can bounce, so they rely on squirrels and
jays to be carried away and buried. Blackberries, apples and haws are
dispersed by being eaten by a bird and passed through its body.

Other forms of animal dispersal are less obvious: ants carry away fruits
of daisy and deadnettle, and goldfinches scatter plantains. Other plants
play a more active part themselves. The seeds of lupins are thrown out by
the twisting of the pod as it opens; the harebell has a sort of pepperpot
mechanism as the flower shakes in the wind. Sycamore 'keys' need no
description, nor do the 'parachutes' of dandelions, except to note that the
'parachutes' only open in dry weather, when conditions are favourable for
flight.

While examining the flowers in the garden, you may notice, even
perhaps with consternation, a pale, barely visible spider sitting in a
yellow or white flower. This is a crab spider. It does not spin a web but lies
in wait for an insect to approach. The spider should be assured of a good
living as insects fly in to sip nectar, but an insect only falls victim if it lands
just in the right position. It must alight within reach of the spider's long
arms, and it must face the spider, then dip its head into the flower in
search of nectar. The spider faces two problems which are always con-

nected with a waiting stratagem. The potential victims may spot the danger and the predator may, itself, fall prey, in this case to birds. Nevertheless, the crab spider's colour, which matches its background, would seem to be ample protection.

It is easy to assume that an animal is camouflaged if we find it hard to see but we have to remember that animals may have eyesight keener than ours, particularly when it is a matter of life and death. Insect eyes are very different from ours and they do not see the same colours, so it would be incorrect to assume that they cannot see the crab spider in its ambush. This can be tested, however. A simple experiment is to arrange a dozen dandelion heads, 30 centimetres (1 foot) apart, on the lawn. Put a yellow pebble the same size as the spider in alternate flowers and put a black pebble in the others. Note which flowers are visited by flying insects. In one experiment, lasting half an hour, eight times as many insects visited the dandelions containing the almost invisible pebbles.

Spiders can often inspire intense revulsion. Even a close-up photograph of a hairy spider can make the flesh creep, which is unfortunate, because spiders are fascinating for the many stratagems which they use to catch their prey.

The main activities of the spiders most likely to be found in your garden have already been described in the chapter on Spiders and Flies, but it is worth admiring again the orb-web of the garden spider; a delight to the eye, its utilitarian construction is a marvel of economy.

An American naturalist, W. M. Barrows, studied orb-web spiders by attaching a bristle to the clapper of an old-fashioned electric bell. The pitch of the bell was adjusted by a screw (although Barrows removed the actual bell for comfort), so that the frequency of the bristle's vibrations could be altered. Sticking the bristle into the web, Barrows was able to discover which frequencies drew a response from the spider. He found that large spiders respond to lower frequency vibrations such as would be produced by bluebottles, while smaller spiders were attracted to the higher frequencies produced by tiny flies. Another naturalist investigated house spiders. He found that high frequencies sent the spiders scuttling for shelter and a handclap caused them to jump off their webs with fright.

Replacing the bristle with a stout piece of wire adapts the electric bell apparatus for examining the hunting behaviour of the greater waterboatmen. Perhaps better known as the backswimmer for obvious reasons, this is a predatory bug, unlike the lesser waterboatman, which swims the right way up and is vegetarian. The backswimmer homes in on its prey by detecting vibrations in the water caused by its movements. First it swings to face the source of disturbance, then it swims rapidly towards it. Then it will cannon headlong into the vibrating wire. It will continue banging its head until it finds that the wire has the wrong taste. Be careful when handling backswimmers: they can nip a finger.

I once heard of a gardener who was plagued by snails. His method of control was simply to throw the snails over the wall. He never got rid of them, because he did not realize that snails can find their way home. The strength of their homing powers can be tested by marking some with paint spots and depositing them at various distances from where they were found. It is best to use those from a 'roost' under a flowerpot or piece of old sacking. Also, look elsewhere to see whether any of the snails have strayed.

If the snails are moving around the garden, the paint marks can be used to calculate the total population. Mark a large number and allow some time to elapse. Then count the proportion which have paint marks in a fairly careful search.

Say that one hundred were painted and you found that twenty-five out of fifty had paint marks in the second search. Then the population in the garden will be $100 \times 50 \div 25 = 200$. Similar experiments can be carried out by marking butterflies and wood-lice.

The smaller invertebrate animals do not lend themselves to experimental work; they usually escape attention altogether. To show

The dandelion is probably not one of the best-loved plants in the average well-kept garden, yet it is a very useful herb and both decorative and interesting as well. Its brilliant yellow flowers are among the first harbingers of spring, and provide nectar and pollen for insects such as drone-flies lured out of hibernation by early sunshine. These insects carry pollen from flower to flower as they feed, and assist in cross-fertilization. For seed dispersal, however, the dandelion relies on the wind. Its seed-heads develop into a fluffy ball of little parachutes, the well-known 'dandelion clock', each parachute attached to a single seed which, when ripe and dry, is borne away by the wind for a considerable distance.

141

Crab spiders do not build webs in which to trap their insect prey, but lurk in flowers, waiting for visiting insects to come to them in search of nectar and pollen. The spiders rest with long front legs held out ready to envelop any insect alighting on the flowers. They are so well matched with their background that even the human-eye, which is much more sensitive than that of an insect, has difficulty in seeing them. In order to blend with a variety of different flowers, crab spiders can change colour from white to yellow or even pink, to match the particular flower in which they are sitting. Often it is the captured prey such as a large fly or butterfly, apparently resting on a flower in an unusual position but actually dead and held by the spider, which gives away the presence of a crab spider in a flower. Like most spiders the female is much larger than her mate, who could well be mistaken for another species; his legs are proportionately much longer and dark, and he has black markings on the abdomen.

the myriads of life forms, the animals need to be collected and identified. The more active animals can be collected in pitfalls, a sealed-down version of the elephant trap. Sink jam jars or plastic yogurt pots into the ground with their rims flush with the surface. A greater selection will be caught if some rotting fruit or meat is put in as a bait, but many animals just topple in without looking where they are going. Some can climb out again, but a little water with detergent added will trap them. It will also drown them, so decide for yourself whether the deaths of some animals, however lowly, are worth the satisfying of your curiosity.

The method of collecting less active animals is also likely to end in their death. These animals can be driven out of a handful of leaf litter or loose soil by the gentle application of heat and light. The simplest apparatus is a kitchen sieve, to hold the sample, with a lamp above. These animals work their way downwards and, slipping through the meshes of the sieve, fall into a bowl of water.

Mammals are a secretive class and not easily observed. Except for the grey squirrel, which is a common inhabitant of gardens, and a weasel or stoat which may run through the flowerbeds, mammals are generally most active at night. Your cat will probably provide samples of what is living in the garden and nests of mice and voles turn up under logs or in sheds. Observing mammals requires considerable patience or good fortune but they can be lured into a suitable viewing place by gifts of food. Hedgehogs like their traditional bread and milk, while the mice and rats like kitchen scraps and grain, but the baiting has to be organized so that cats and birds do not get it first. Once the mammals are making an appearance, which can be checked by their footprints appearing in a dusting of flour or fine sand, keep watch with a light. A red light is always recommended but, as the mammals become tame, they will get used to a white one. The ultimate in garden-mammal watching is to have foxes or badgers feeding in the light streaming from the windows.

A CHAPTER COULD be written about projects on birds. They are the most easily seen, most familiar and most admired of all animals. Much can be learnt by keeping a diary of events in the birds' year. Migrants appear and disappear. Song bursts forth in earnest during early spring, dies away in summer and recommences at a lower intensity in late August. Nesting and rearing the brood follows the age-old pattern, but these should be observed at a distance because examination of nests may lead to desertion or predation. Instead, calculate the frequency with which the adult birds bring food to the nest. A brood of growing youngsters with ever-gaping beaks keeps the parents busy throughout the day. A few simple sums, with the aid of a book for information on clutch size and time spent by chicks in the nest, will give a rough idea of how many collecting trips the parents make to rear a family, how much food each chick gets and what effect this may have on the garden's insects.

A varied garden will provide information on the diet of the birds.

Even similar species have different preferences. Blackbirds eat more fruit than song thrushes and the latter hammer open snails on 'anvils' (look for the remains of your marked snails). The tits feed on different parts of a tree and the diets of finches range from the cracking of cherry stones by the secretive hawfinch to the nibbling of thistle seeds by the goldfinch.

Finally, everyone should, at some time in their life, take the trouble to get up early, or stay up late, and witness the dawn chorus, when the air rings with bird song. Who starts the chorus, and how long is each bird's part? Does the chorus start earlier on fine days?

Nearly all the animals mentioned in this chapter are likely to be found in the garden, even if it is buried in a city far from the country. The proviso is, of course, that the garden contains a variety of plants, both herbaceous and shrubs, to provide homes and shelter. Naturally the variety will be greater in the country where the animals can move in more easily and, to an extent, the fauna of a garden reflects the nature of the countryside. My first house was in Argyll, in Scotland, and I grew accustomed to visits by sparrowhawks and buzzards, dippers and woodcocks. Then I moved into the fields of Cambridgeshire and became familiar with yellowhammers and skylarks, kestrels and rooks. Of course, these birds were visitors rather than residents but, as far as lesser creatures are concerned, the garden is often a richer habitat than the surrounding countryside. At the extremes, where a garden is surrounded by moorland or modern 'prairie' farms, or in a town, it is a veritable oasis of wildlife.

Agriculture and horticulture are, in essence, the shifting of the balance of nature for human purposes. By ploughing or digging, spraying or weeding, the farmer and gardener make sure that certain plants thrive at the expense of others. The favoured species are the crops or show plants of the garden and the others are weeds. A weed is simply a plant growing where it is not wanted and classing plants as

weeds depends on your point of view. Poppies are pests in a wheatfield but not in a garden border. The same distinction holds true for animals. Those which attack the favoured plants are pests, but the pigeon fancier has an attitude to his birds which conflicts with the views of the pea-grower. It is all a matter of opinion and that of the gardener is that anything which impedes the perfect growth of roses, cabbages or plums is to be eradicated. He can quite easily divide the animals in the garden into 'friends' or 'enemies', depending on whether they eat his plants or not. Unfortunately, it is difficult to eradicate enemies without harming friends, and a horticultural paradise is likely to be rather devoid of wildlife. On the other hand, a garden dedicated to being a nature reserve is liable to draw complaints from neighbours about the danger of spreading weeds. Compromise is, as always, an acceptable solution.

The two basic rules for encouraging wildlife in the garden are: be sparing with chemicals and do not be over-tidy.

It would try the patience of a saint to see his cabbages being devastated by caterpillars without raising a finger against them but the temptation to saturate them with the most powerful available poison should be controlled. The most toxic and long-lasting of pesticides and weed-killers are disappearing and being replaced by more benign substances, such as weed-killers which kill only those plants they contact and are inactivated when they touch the ground. For insect pests, pyrethrum and derris, which are extracted from tropical plants, and Bordeaux mixture (quick lime and copper sulphate in solution) will not harm higher forms of life. Soapy water will wash off aphids when they are easily accessible but more toxic substances can be used with care on the worst infestations, not, for instance, when the wind will spread the poison. The organophosphorus compounds such as malathion break down rapidly, unlike the persistent DDT, which has been withdrawn from garden use. They are not likely to harm birds and mammals but will destroy useful insects and spiders.

Experiments on the use of alternative methods of pest control which do not use poisons or which keep the killing agent well under control have shown encouraging results. The Henry Doubleday Research Association has carried out experiments which are adaptable to gardens. They used baited traps to attract such pests as the pernicious carrot fly, the onion fly, cabbage root fly and others. As they travel in search of plants in which to lay their eggs, these insects feed on the pollen of umbellifer plants, which include garden carrots, parsley, wild cow parsley, hemlock and hogweed. The traps are jars containing a 10 per cent brown sugar solution and a 5 millimetre ($\frac{3}{16}$ inch) mesh to keep out bees. They are baited with coriander oil or synthetic apple blossom, and placed in a sheltered place in mid-May so as to intercept the flies as they approach the crops.

The Association also recommends some of the old remedies. Apple blossom weevils crawl down the trunks of apple and pear trees to hibernate and strips of sacking tied around the trunk form an acceptable winter home. Take them off and burn them in October. Grease bands applied to trunks and stems from autumn to spring trap wingless female winter moths and others as they ascend to lay their eggs. Leatherjackets, the larvae of craneflies or daddy-long-legs, kill grass by eating the roots. Water the lawn and cover with a sheet of black polythene. This draws the pupae to the surface. Roll or mow to kill them, and give the birds a treat.

The compromise on neatness is easy to maintain because it is a good excuse to be a little lazy. A few weeds allowed to seed, a corner left undisturbed where stinging nettles, docks and thistles, can support a crop of caterpillars, and plants allowed to run to seed, these signs of neglect will be appreciated by insects and birds alike. Leave a few brambles in a hedge so that the flowers will attract ringlet and gatekeeper butterflies, and delay trimming the privet. A well-kept

Hedgehogs are probably more common in gardens than is sometimes supposed, but being nocturnal they are not often observed. They mostly feed on the great variety of small animal prey such as slugs, earthworms and beetles. They will also occasionally eat fruit such as the odd strawberry or windfall apple or plum. With such catholic tastes almost any food put out for them will command their attention: tinned cat or dog-food, meat scraps, bacon rind or cake. But traditionally the pet hedgehog is most likely to be offered a saucer of bread and milk. He certainly appreciates this dish enough to learn to come regularly for it, and in time he becomes tame enough not to flinch and curl up at the approach of the thoughtful human donor.

privet hedge is as boring as a boarded fence, but leave it to grow until late summer and it produces tiny pale flowers. These are a great attraction to butterflies and bumble bees.

WILDLIFE CAN BE attracted in a more positive fashion by planning a garden. There are several cultivated plants which are particularly attractive to insects and their different flowering times give a continuous supply of nectar. Especially favoured are aubrieta, honesty, alyssum, lavender, petunia, buddleia, ice plant and Michaelmas daisy. The old-fashioned plants of the cottage garden are better than modern highly-bred strains where nectar and scent have lost out to size and shape.

Other insects can be attracted by giving them homes. An old log provides a 'total environment' for many insects and other invertebrates—worms, wood-lice, centipedes and spiders. As it rots, colourful shows of fungi appear and wither, and boring beetles like the stag beetle, whose males have huge pincer-like jaws, lay eggs and leave their larvae to burrow through the wood. Suitable houses for earwigs can be made by stuffing an upturned flowerpot with newspaper. Without the newspaper, a pile of flowerpots usually attracts garden snails. The versatile flowerpot can be adapted for use by bumble bees, when buried upside down with the small drain-hole left as an entrance. The chances of a queen bumble bee taking up residence and founding a colony there are enhanced if the shredded grass from an old mouse nest is added, because deserted mouse nests are a popular place for bumble bees to colonize. Indeed, suitable boxes or other containers can be put out in the undergrowth for mice to build their winter nests and so become attractive to bumble bees in the following spring.

Making provision for earwigs and bumble bees may raise a few eyebrows among the neighbours but attracting birds to the garden is an accepted pastime. From tossing crusts into the backyard to the most elaborate bird tables, feeding the birds gives pleasure to millions and there has been no shortage of advice published to foster the practice. The simplest arrangement for feeding birds, after throwing scraps out of the back door, is a basic bird table—a pole and a plank nailed to the top of it. Increasing sophistication is added by a raised rim to prevent food being blown off, leaving gaps for rain to run off and remnants of food to be cleared away. A roof deflects rain and snow; various feeders can be hung about, and all sorts of proprietary foods and home-made mixes put out to attract the greatest variety of birds. Remember that some birds shun bird tables. Blackbirds will be happier foraging on the ground underneath and wrens may be persuaded to take cheese crumbs scattered under low bushes. Berry-bearing bushes can be worked into the garden plan alongside insect-attracting plants. Hawthorn, barberry, cotoneaster, ivy, holly and rowan all provide both food and shelter and the small birds like the seeds of dock, thistles, and groundsel, if you can leave these plants unweeded.

The corpse of a dead animal – a bird or a mammal – attracts a number of insects to feed on it. The first to arrive are usually the flies, like the greenbottle and flesh fly. The greenbottle lays its eggs on the corpse and they hatch into maggots, but the eggs of the flesh fly hatch inside the parent's body and the maggots are born alive. The maggots burrow their way into the flesh and liquefy it with their digestive juices. After a few days, the maggots pupate in a hard brown cylinder and the adults soon emerge.

The rove beetle and its relative, the devil's coach horse, are fast-running beetles which are identified by the short wingcases which look like a waistcoat. These beetles can be mistaken for earwigs but they do not have 'forceps' at the end of the abdomen. Rove beetles eat decaying flesh and prey on maggots and other larvae living in the corpse.

The scarab shown here has no common name, but it is related to the dor beetles. It feeds on the bodies of small animals. The striking burying or sexton beetles are so-named because they bury small carcasses before laying their eggs. The male and female work together and dig away the soil under the body so that it sinks into the ground. The eggs are laid by the body and the female beetle remains with them and feeds the larvae by regurgitating food until they can manage the flesh for themselves.

146

Nest boxes are another provision for attracting birds to the garden and substantive advice on this subject is given on page 33. With the preoccupation for giving birds food and shelter, it is often forgotten that they also need water. As well as providing drinking water for birds in frost or drought, much pleasure can be had by providing water for birds to bathe in. Bowls, upturned dustbin lids, anything will do.

Garden ponds are also useful in attracting and keeping bird life in your garden. A simple method of making your own pond is described and illustrated on pages 52 and 53. If it is possible, always try to have a shallow end for birds, with a ramp or slope somewhere so that hedgehogs and mice which inadvertently fall in may climb to safety and froglets can emerge into adulthood. A deeper section should offer shelter for fishes, amphibians and water insects and could also be stocked with water plants grown in flower pots.

For the naturalist, the garden pond is most useful as a reserve for wild animals brought in from countryside ponds and lakes. Some will probably arrive by themselves. Dragonflies and damselflies are particularly exciting visitors. The large hawker dragonflies travel some distance from water when hunting. They visit the driest gardens and may stay to breed in garden ponds. Pond snails are useful creatures to bring into the pond and can be surprisingly active and interesting to watch. Fish have to be introduced with some caution if you want to keep the smaller animals, because ponds, like the rest of the garden, have to be managed by tipping the balance of nature in the direction you want.

SUITABLY MANAGED, the garden can provide recreation for horticulturalist and naturalist at the same time. The two are probably combined in the same person but what about the increasingly important character, the conservationist? The garden is now recognized as an important refuge of wildlife. On one hand, the countryside in some places is becoming less diverse: acre upon acre of barley or sugar beet or sitka spruce. On the other hand, the cities are spreading. In suburban areas, pockets of countryside often remain and housing areas with mature gardens represent a broken countryside of scattered copses and hedges. Within this habitat, badgers can linger in secluded places to emerge at night and dig for worms on lawns; foxes positively thrive, denning up under garden sheds and raiding dustbins. Overhead there are owls and bats. Garden plants and bird tables support a large and diverse population of birds, especially of those species which naturally live in woodland edges, where they can forage in open country.

These are instances of animals surviving because the garden is rather like their original home, but there are a few examples of changes in behaviour allowing birds to come into gardens. Siskins have taken to eating peanuts, reed buntings attend bird tables in winter; but a few blackcaps have actually stopped migrating because bird tables provide them with an alternative winter food. Even more welcome is the value

Starlings are noisy and gregarious birds that should be encouraged in the garden because of the fine job they do in consuming large quantities of leatherjackets and other pests. Not only should food be put out to sustain and encourage birds through the winter, but a bowl of water should be offered as well. During frosty weather the water must be renewed frequently, for birds can become just as thirsty at such times as during a summer drought. On milder days, or even on frosty ones, birds love to bathe, and provide us with an entertaining spectacle. The provision of water during the soft fruit season may benefit ourselves as well as the birds, for thirsty birds are more likely to eat quantities of juicy fruit if they cannot readily find drinking water.

of gardens in preserving species. There is nothing in Britain to equal the revival of the American blackbird. It was fast disappearing because the trees and stumps where it nested were cleared away but it is now recovering through the systematic provision of thousands of nest boxes. The nearest we can achieve is the increasing reliance on garden ponds by the common frog, which has become anything but common in many places. Nevertheless, the British love of gardens may well become the saving of British wildlife in a world where wild places are fast disappearing.

Index

Bibliography

Linda Bennett *RSPB Book of Garden Birds*, Hamlyn 1978
Maurice Burton *Wild Animals of the British Isles*, Frederick Warne 1968
Robert Burton *Ponds: their wildlife and upkeep*, David & Charles 1977
Michael Chinery *The Family Naturalist*, Macdonald and Janes 1977
A. D. Imms *Insect Natural History*, new edition Collins 1971
Dr Denis Owen *Towns and Gardens*, Hodder & Stoughton 1978
Tony Soper *The New Bird Table Book*, David & Charles 1973
Michael Tweedie *Pleasure from Insects*, David & Charles 1968
The Oxford Book of Insects, Oxford University Press 1979